Love to Cook

Love to Cook

Mary Berry

BOOKS

Contents

Introduction

I really do love to cook. For me, cooking is never a chore – I find it relaxing after a busy day to potter in the kitchen, putting together something delicious to eat. And it's always wonderful to share food with friends and family, even if, as has happened during this last year of lockdown, you have to leave it on their doorstep! Making this book has been a joy. It's so good to be able to include some of my favourite dishes, things I go back to time and time again, plus new recipes I wanted to try and fresh discoveries I've made. We began this project just before the first lockdown, so we had to adjust to a very different way of working. Of course, we all had to be cooking in our own homes and so we delivered dishes to each other to taste and discuss on Zoom. Strange though it was, we did have much more time than usual to spend on each recipe – all the time in the world, in fact, as there wasn't much else to do! Somehow or other we managed, and I actually did more cooking than ever. Being able to freeze food was a great help and made me doubly keen to get plenty of advice on freezing into this book. We all have busy lives and being able to get ahead and batch cook is such a time saver. I've added a note to every recipe as to whether it can be frozen or not. For instance, I've included a range of different burgers – not just beef, but pork, lamb, salmon and even a vegan burger. All freeze beautifully; just wrap them individually and you can pop one out of the freezer for a speedy supper. Sometimes, though, you want an easy meal that you can prepare quickly and serve up at once, and some of my Asian-inspired recipes are perfect for these moments – dishes such as Prawn and Wild Mushroom Stir Fry on page 47 and Hoisin Chicken with Cashews on page 67 can be ready with very little effort.

Enjoying cooking means avoiding stress in the kitchen, so I do like to do some preparation ahead of time. When I have people coming round to eat, I am particularly keen to get as much done in advance as possible so I can enjoy their company later on. You'll find lots of suggestions for getting ahead and great ideas like my Magical Prepare Ahead Platter of Vegetables on page 180, which allows you to make a great range of vegetable accompaniments in advance and reheat them at the last minute – without ending up in a sea of pots and pans! I also love dishes such as the Slow Roast Lamb on page 126, which you can pop in the oven and leave to cook for hours – smelling delicious – while you relax with your friends and family. I've included plenty of one-pot dishes as well, which everyone enjoys, as they save time and effort but are so good to eat – try my Spanish Hot Pot on page 100 and my Double Mushroom Stroganoff on page 148.

I always encourage people to take my recipes and experiment with them. Perhaps you've made the Salmon and Dill Burgers on page 57 and thought how lovely they would be as tiny fish cakes to dip into the caper mayo and serve with drinks? Don't be afraid to try out your ideas. And when you have made something successfully, think about putting one of those little sticky notes on that page of the book, saying how the quantity fitted perfectly in the brown earthenware dish you got for Christmas, for example, or how a certain recipe was particularly popular with a favourite friend.

I am increasingly conscious of environmental concerns and do my best to cut down on waste. When I make a Sunday roast, I am careful never to throw away leftover gravy – instead, I stash it in the freezer to serve with sausages or to incorporate in a shepherd's pie. I find that having a plan for the week's meals helps avoid food waste. Keep a regular check on your fridge and stock cupboard and see what needs using up. If, for example, you have some veg that are starting to look a bit tired, make a delicious vegetable curry, such as the Roasted Vegetable and Coconut Curry on page 151, or soup for a quick lunch. I'm also eating meat less often nowadays, and making sure I choose good meat when I do serve it, preferably from a butcher or farm shop. I reuse plastic containers and I love those beeswax wraps for covering leftovers.

In this book you will find 'For the Love of …' sections, with tips and advice on some of my favourite things. Wonderful fresh ingredients, like fruit, herbs and vegetables, are such an important part of my recipes and it is lovely to grow a few things yourself if you possibly can. I nearly always use fresh herbs, as they are so much better than dried in most instances, and I have pots by the kitchen door. Even if you don't have a garden, herbs are the easiest things to grow on a balcony or windowsill and they add so much flavour and freshness to your cooking. And don't stop with herbs! You can grow many kinds of vegetables in pots, growbags, even dustbins, if you have a little outside space. It is so satisfying to pick your own tomatoes, beans or berries and cook them for supper.

As always, I've kept my recipes as simple as possible, not too many ingredients, no special equipment and no complicated techniques. I can't see the point of including extra processes when you can do something quickly and easily. And you'll find a glorious photo of every single recipe to whet your appetite and see the presentation we like. I very much hope that this book helps you enjoy your time in the kitchen. I believe that if you love to cook, everyone will love your cooking!

Mary Berry

For the Love
of...a Store Cupboard

My larder at home is a treasure trove of essential ingredients that can be used either as the building blocks of a bake, like flour, or as the small but critical flavourings in a dish, like my jars of whole spices and pastes. There are certain items I would never be without, like sunflower and olive oil, and others that are far too useful to miss out, such as dried pasta or puy lentils. With these ingredients at hand, and a few fresh ones from the fridge, you will be able to turn a simple vegetable or main ingredient into a sensational supper, conjure up a tray of biscuits, or transform something ordinary into something special.

Baking

Almond extract

Baking powder and bicarbonate of soda

Chocolate – good-quality dark and white

Cocoa powder

Cornflour

Flour – plain and self-raising

Sugar – caster, demerara, icing
and light muscovado

Vanilla extract

Grains

Couscous

Lentils – puy and red

Oats

Panko breadcrumbs

Pasta – penne and linguine or spaghetti

Pearl barley

Quinoa

Noodles – egg and rice

Rice – basmati, jasmine and risotto

Nuts, seeds and dried fruit

Almonds – whole, flaked and ground

Dried apricots and dates

Pumpkin seeds

Raisins and sultanas

Sesame seeds

Oils and vinegars

Oil – olive and sunflower

Vinegar – white wine, balsamic and rice

Herbs and spices

Bay leaves

Black peppercorns

Ground spices – chilli powder, cumin,
coriander, cinnamon, ginger, mixed
spice, paprika and turmeric

Stock cubes – chicken, vegetable and beef

Table salt and sea salt flakes

Whole spices – cardamom pods,
cinnamon sticks, nutmeg and star anise

Condiments

Apricot jam

Hoisin sauce

Honey (runny)

Horseradish sauce

Lemon curd

Mayonnaise

Mustard – English, Dijon, grainy and powder

Redcurrant jelly

Soy sauce

Sun-dried tomato paste

Sweet chilli sauce

Thai fish sauce

Tomato ketchup

Tomato purée

White miso paste

Worcestershire sauce

Tinned and preserved foods

Beans – butter and cannellini

Capers

Chickpeas

Chopped tomatoes

Coconut milk

Dill-pickled cucumber

Gherkins

Olives

Passata

Preserved lemons

Roasted peppers

Recipe Finder by Style

FIRST
COURSES

Balsamic Beetroot, Quail's Egg and Smoked Fish Plate

Serves 4

You can use your preferred smoked fish, but gravadlax is my favourite. Smoked salmon, smoked trout and smoked mackerel would work well, too.

6 quail's eggs

150g (5oz) cooked beetroot, cut into tiny dice

250g (9oz) gravadlax (about 8 slices)

80g (3oz) lamb's lettuce

Celery salt, to taste

Balsamic glaze, to garnish

Olive oil, to garnish

Mustard Sauce

3 tbsp crème fraîche

2 tsp creamed hot horseradish sauce

2 tsp grainy mustard

2 tbsp chopped dill, plus extra to garnish

½ tsp caster sugar

....

Mary's tips

* *Can be assembled on individual plates or a platter up to 6 hours ahead. Dress just before serving.*

* *Not for freezing.*

Place the quail's eggs in a small saucepan, cover with cold water and bring to the boil. Boil for 3 minutes, then drain and run under cold water. Peel and slice each one in half.

Measure all the mustard sauce ingredients into a bowl. Mix well and season with salt and black pepper.

Divide the diced beetroot between four plates. Place the gravadlax slices next to the beetroot, and the lamb's lettuce next to the gravadlax. Arrange 3 halves of egg alongside, then sprinkle them with celery salt and black pepper. Spoon some sauce on to each plate.

Just before serving, drizzle the balsamic glaze and olive oil over the beetroot and lamb's lettuce, and garnish with sprigs of dill.

Thai Vegetable Rice Wraps

Makes 36 wraps

These are an impressive canapé for when you're cooking for a crowd and you really want to spoil your guests with something different. The vegetables are cut into fine strips the length of a matchstick. Rice paper wrappers can be bought easily by mail order, at some supermarkets or from specialist delis.

1 medium carrot, peeled and very thinly sliced into strips 5cm (2in) long

¼ cucumber, deseeded and very thinly sliced into strips 5cm (2in) long

½ red pepper, deseeded and very thinly sliced into strips 5cm (2in) long

½ bunch of coriander, chopped

12 rice paper spring roll wrappers (about 22cm/ 8½in diameter)

Olive oil, for greasing

Large bunch of Thai basil leaves

Dipping Sauce

2 tbsp sweet chilli sauce

2 tbsp white wine vinegar

1½ tbsp soy sauce

¼ red chilli, deseeded and diced

1 garlic clove, crushed

½ tsp sesame oil (optional)

½ bunch of coriander, chopped

....

Mary's tips

* *Wraps can be made up to 6 hours ahead.*

* *Not for freezing.*

Place the carrot, cucumber, pepper and coriander in a large bowl and toss together.

To make the dipping sauce, place all the ingredients except the coriander in a bowl and mix well. Spoon 1 tablespoon of the sauce on to the vegetables in the large bowl and toss until coated. Pour the remaining sauce into a small serving bowl and add the coriander.

Fill a shallow dish with warm water and lightly oil a large plate. Working with one wrapper at a time, place a wrapper in the water and soak for a few seconds until it is soft. Transfer to a flat plate. Place a small pile of vegetables in the centre of the wrapper. Place a basil leaf on top and fold in the sides. Fold the top over the veg then continue to roll up tightly to make a long cigar shape. Place on the oiled large plate and cover with damp kitchen paper. Repeat with the remaining wrappers and vegetables. Place in the fridge until you are ready to serve.

Slice each wrap into three and arrange cut side up on a large platter. Serve with the dipping sauce.

Prawn, Mango, Smoked Salmon and Avocado Sharing Platter

Serves 4–6

Perfect for eating outdoors in summer, this looks stunning, is quick to assemble and is a joy to share. Peppadew peppers add colour and a little heat and are available in jars.

6 tbsp mayonnaise

1 tbsp ketchup

1 tbsp creamed hot horseradish sauce

1 tbsp sun-dried tomato paste

350g (12oz) small, cooked prawns, drained and dried on kitchen paper

100g (4oz) rocket leaves

1 ripe avocado, peeled and sliced into thin strips

1 ripe mango, peeled and sliced into thin strips

4–6 slices smoked salmon

Peppadew and Mustard Dressing

2 tsp Dijon mustard

Juice of ½ lemon

1 tsp caster sugar

6 tbsp olive oil

2 mild Peppadew peppers, finely chopped

Mary's tips

* *Prawns can be mixed in the sauce and the salad can be assembled up to 4 hours ahead. Add the avocado just before serving.*

* *Not for freezing.*

Measure the mayonnaise, ketchup, horseradish and sun-dried tomato paste into a small bowl. Season with salt and black pepper and mix well. Stir in the prawns, then spoon into a small serving bowl and place on a platter.

Place the rocket in a bowl on the platter. Arrange two piles of avocado, two piles of mango and the smoked salmon around the bowls. Season with ground black pepper.

Measure all the dressing ingredients into a small jug and whisk well. Toss the rocket in some of the dressing and drizzle a little over the platter ingredients.

Serve with crusty bread.

Watermelon, Parma Ham and Asparagus Posh Plates

Serves 6

When entertaining friends at home, I love to have a 'posh plate' in the fridge ready for serving as a starter, made ahead and out of the way. This is perfect and so delicious, too. Remoulade is a favourite and I have it as a salad instead of coleslaw. Watermelons are now available the size of a very large grapefruit or pomelo which, when sliced in an individual round, makes a perfect base for a single portion.

1 very small watermelon
18 asparagus tips
12 slices Parma ham
6 lemon wedges
Balsamic glaze, to drizzle
Olive oil, to drizzle

Celeriac Remoulade
300g (11oz) peeled celeriac
Juice of 1 lemon
4 heaped tbsp mayonnaise
1 heaped tsp Dijon mustard
Dash of caster sugar

Mary's tips

* *The asparagus tips should be al dente – thick asparagus spears will take about 3 minutes to cook but thinner ones will take less time.*

* *Can be assembled up to 6 hours ahead. Add balsamic glaze and olive oil to serve.*

* *Not for freezing.*

To make the remoulade, finely shred the celeriac into very thin matchsticks. Place in a bowl with half the lemon juice and 100ml (3½fl oz) water to stop the celeriac from discolouring. Measure the remaining lemon juice, the mayonnaise, mustard and sugar into a bowl. Mix well and season with salt and black pepper. Drain the celeriac and dry on kitchen paper. Add to the mayonnaise mixture and coat well. Cover and leave in the fridge for 30 minutes, or longer to soften.

Slice 6 slices (each about 2cm/¾in) from the watermelon. Using a 9cm (3½in) round cutter, stamp out 6 circles from the flesh of the melon. Remove any black seeds.

Blanch the asparagus tips in boiling salted water for about 3 minutes, or until al dente. Drain and refresh under cold water, then drain again.

Place a circle of watermelon on one side of a plate. Spoon some celeriac remoulade next to it. Arrange two slices of Parma ham in a swirl on another side. Arrange the asparagus tips between the watermelon and the Parma ham. Add a wedge of lemon and drizzle the balsamic glaze and olive oil around the edge of the plate. Repeat to make 6 plates.

Sprinkle with salt and black pepper to serve.

Cheesey Quiche Bites

Makes 48 bites

The joy of these bites is that the Parmesan pastry is only on the base – the outside crust is trimmed off to make neat squares. They are the perfect nibble for when friends come round. If you are making these ahead, freeze the quiche uncut but carefully wrapped and defrost when needed. Cut into 24 small squares, arrange them close together on a baking sheet and reheat for 10 minutes at 160°C/140°C fan/Gas 3. Set a timer so that they don't overcook! Cut into triangles to serve.

Parmesan Pastry

175g (6oz) plain flour

75g (3oz) butter, cubed

25g (1oz) Parmesan,
   finely grated

1 large egg, beaten

2 tbsp water

Quiche Filling

2 tbsp sunflower oil

2 onions, finely chopped

2 large eggs, beaten

250ml (9fl oz) double cream

2 tbsp chopped basil

175g (6oz) blue cheese,
   coarsely grated

50g (2oz) mature Cheddar,
   coarsely grated

You will need a 23 × 30cm
   (9 × 12in) Swiss roll tin.

Mary's tips

* *Can be made up to a day
ahead and reheated to serve.*

* *Freezes well cooked.*

To make the pastry, measure the flour, butter, Parmesan and a pinch of salt into a food processor and whiz until the mixture resembles breadcrumbs. Add the beaten egg and water and whiz again until the pastry comes together into a ball. Alternatively, rub the flour, butter, Parmesan and a pinch of salt together in a mixing bowl with your fingertips before adding the beaten egg and water.

Roll the pastry out on a lightly floured work surface to a thin rectangle slightly larger than the tin. Carefully transfer the pastry to the tin, pressing it across the base and up the sides, and leaving an overhang of pastry. Prick the sides and base with a fork and place in the fridge to chill for 30 minutes.

Preheat the oven to 200°C/180°C fan/Gas 6.

Line the pastry case with non-stick baking paper and baking beans, slide into the oven and bake blind for 15 minutes. Remove the paper and beans and bake for another 5 minutes or until pale golden and crisp and dry.

Meanwhile, place the oil in a frying pan over a medium heat. Add the onion and fry for a few minutes, then cover with a lid, reduce the heat and cook for about 15 minutes until soft.

Remove the lid and drive off any liquid over a high heat, then set aside to cool.

Reduce the oven temperature to 180°C/160°C fan/Gas 4.

Beat the eggs and double cream together in a jug and season with salt and black pepper.

Spread the onion evenly over the base of the pastry. Scatter the basil and blue cheese on top, then pour in the egg mixture. Sprinkle with the Cheddar and bake in the oven for about 20 minutes, until the filling is set and lightly golden on top.

When ready to serve, trim off the outside edges of the pastry. Divide the quiche into 24 squares by cutting in 6 along the long edge and 4 across the short edge. Slice each square in half to make triangles.

Serve warm.

Twice Baked Crab Soufflés

Serves 6

Such a rich, decadent first course or lunch. Fresh crab meat makes a huge difference to the dish.

25g (1oz) butter, plus
    extra for greasing

25g (1oz) plain flour

200ml (⅓ pint) hot milk

3 tbsp creamed hot
    horseradish (or
    2 tbsp creamed hot
    horseradish sauce)

1 tbsp chopped dill

2 eggs, separated

200g (7oz) fresh
    white crab meat

300ml (½ pint) pouring
    double cream

2 tsp grated fresh root ginger

1 × 70g packet brown shrimp

You will need a 8 × 100ml
    (3½fl oz) or 6 × 150ml
    (¼ pint) ramekins.

Mary's tips

* *Lining the tin with kitchen paper helps to stabilise the ramekins in the bain marie.*

* *Adding ginger and horseradish to the cream will cause it to thicken, so make sure you add them just before pouring around the soufflés.*

* *The soufflés can be cooked 6 hours ahead. Reheat with the cream sauce to serve.*

* *Not for freezing.*

Preheat the oven to 220°C/200°C fan/Gas 7. Grease the bases and sides of the ramekins with butter. Line a small roasting tin with a piece of kitchen paper and sit the ramekins on top.

Melt the butter in a saucepan over a medium heat. Add the flour and stir for a few seconds. Whisk in the hot milk and continue to whisk until you have a smooth, thickened sauce. Remove from the heat. Leave to cool slightly.

Add 1 tablespoon of the horseradish, the dill and egg yolks to the pan. Season with salt and black pepper, then stir in the crab meat.

Whisk the egg white in a large clean bowl until stiff like cloud. Gently fold the whites into the crab mixture. Divide evenly between the ramekins.

Place the ramekins in the roasting tin, then half fill the tin with boiling water to make a bain marie. Place the tin in the oven and bake for 15–20 minutes, or until well risen and lightly golden on top. Leave to cool.

When you are ready to serve the soufflés, preheat the oven to 200°C/180°C fan/Gas 6 and butter a shallow ovenproof dish. Run a palette knife around the edges of the ramekins to release the soufflés, then carefully place them in the ovenproof dish.

Mix the cream, ginger and the remaining horseradish in a jug. Season then pour the sauce around the soufflés. Spoon a little pile of shrimp on top of each soufflé. Bake in the oven for 12–15 minutes, or until bubbling around the edges.

Serve hot with bread or salad.

Golden Bruschetta
with Three Toppings

Makes 4

I think bruschetta makes a brilliant starter, lunch or tasty canapé, if cut into small bites. Choosing what to serve on top is up to you, but here are three of our favourites. I find ciabatta is the best type of bread to use as the shape and texture is perfect; however, sourdough or French baguette would work well, too.

3 tbsp olive oil

1 garlic clove, crushed

1 tbsp finely chopped parsley

¼ large ciabatta loaf, cut into 4 × 1cm (½in) slices

Avocado and Pancetta

4 rashers of pancetta

2 ripe avocados, peeled and mashed

Juice of ½ lemon

or

Smoked Salmon, Crème Fraîche and Beetroot

4 tbsp full-fat crème fraîche

2 tbsp chopped dill

100g (4oz) smoked salmon slices

1 small cooked beetroot, diced

Juice of ½ lemon

or

Spiced Brown Shrimp

A knob of butter

100g (4oz) cooked and peeled small brown shrimp

Grating of nutmeg

2 spring onions, thinly sliced

2 tbsp mayonnaise

Juice of ½ small lemon

Preheat the grill to high.

Measure the oil, crushed garlic and parsley into a bowl and stir to combine. Spread this over one side of each slice of bread. Place the bread under the grill and cook for 1–2 minutes on each side, until tinged brown and crisp.

Remove from the grill and leave to cool.

To make the avocado and pancetta topping, place the pancetta in a frying pan over a medium heat and fry for 2–3 minutes, or until crispy and golden. Remove from the pan, drain on kitchen paper and snip into small pieces. Place the mashed avocado in a small bowl and add the lemon juice. Season with salt and black pepper and mix well. Divide the avocado between the slices of grilled ciabatta, then top with the pieces of pancetta to serve.

To make the smoked salmon and beetroot topping, spread the crème fraîche over the slices of grilled ciabatta, then top each one with the dill and a swirl of smoked salmon. Scatter over the diced beetroot and squeeze over the lemon juice. Season with black pepper to serve.

To make the brown shrimp topping, place the butter, shrimp, nutmeg and spring onions in a pan over a medium heat. Cook for 2 minutes, until the shrimp mixture is hot. Spread the mayonnaise over the grilled ciabatta, then spoon the shrimp mixture on top. Squeeze over the lemon juice and season with sea salt flakes and black pepper to serve.

Watercress and Basil Soup

Serves 4–6

There is a wonderful colour to this soup, and it is full of goodness.
The celeriac can be replaced with potato, if you prefer.

A knob of butter

2 medium onions,
  roughly chopped

450g (1lb) peeled
  celeriac, chopped

1 litre (1¾ pints)
  chicken stock

1 tbsp redcurrant jelly

200g (7oz) watercress,
  roughly chopped

Small bunch of
  basil, chopped

Mary's tips

* *Can be made up to a
day ahead.*

* *Freezes well.*

* *If reheating, bring to the
boil and serve at once. If
simmered for too long it
loses its bright green colour.*

Place the butter in a deep saucepan over a medium heat.
Add the onions and fry for a few minutes. Add the celeriac,
stir into the onions and fry for about 2 minutes.

Pour in the stock and stir in the jelly. Cover with a lid and
bring up to the boil. Reduce the heat and simmer gently for
about 25 minutes, or until the vegetables are tender.

Remove from the heat and add the watercress and basil.
Blend with a hand blender or place in a food processor and
whiz until smooth. Season well with salt and black pepper.

Serve hot with crusty bread and a swirl of cream, if you like.

Vegetable Noodle Soup Bowl

Serves 6

Super healthy and light, this soup is packed with goodness and is ideal
for a light lunch or as a first course preceding an oriental main.

1.8 litres (3¼ pints) good
  vegetable stock

5cm (2in) fresh root ginger,
  peeled and grated

1 red chilli, deseeded
  and finely chopped

6 spring onions, sliced

1½ tsp Chinese five
  spice powder

1 tbsp light muscovado sugar

1 tbsp sweet chilli sauce

1 tbsp soy sauce

150g (5oz) shiitake
  mushrooms, sliced

50g (2oz) fine egg noodles

1 pak choi, sliced

Juice of ½ small lime

Small bunch of
  coriander, chopped

Mary's tips

* *Can be made up to a day
  ahead – add the noodles and
  pak choi just before serving.*

* *Not for freezing.*

Pour the stock into a large saucepan and bring up
to the boil.

Add the ginger, chilli, spring onions, Chinese five
spice powder, sugar, sweet chilli sauce and soy sauce,
reduce the heat and simmer gently for 5 minutes.

Add the mushrooms and noodles and simmer for
3–4 minutes until the noodles are cooked. Stir in the
pak choi and lime juice and check the seasoning.
Simmer for a further 2 minutes.

Ladle into bowls and sprinkle with coriander to serve.

Broccoli and Stilton Soup

Serves 4–6

Perfect for using leftover Stilton or blue cheese, this is an inexpensive and warming
winter lunch. If you like truffle oil, you could swirl a little over the top to serve.
We are not too keen on truffles, but I know that many people love them!

50g (2oz) butter

1 large onion, roughly
chopped

350g (12oz) peeled potatoes,
cut into 3cm (1¼in) cubes

1.5 litres (2½ pints) chicken
or vegetable stock

350g (12oz) broccoli, cut
into small florets

100g (4oz) Stilton,
coarsely grated

Mary's tips

* *Can be made a day
ahead and reheated.*

* *Freezes well but may lose
its bright green colour.*

Place the butter in a large saucepan over a high heat. Add
the onion and fry for a few minutes, then stir in the potatoes
and stock. Season with salt and black pepper, cover with a
lid and bring up to the boil. Reduce the heat and simmer
for 15 minutes.

Add the broccoli, increase the heat and boil gently for about
5 minutes, or until the broccoli is just tender.

Remove from the heat and blend with a hand blender or
whiz in a food processor until smooth.

Add the Stilton, return to the heat and stir until the cheese
is just melted.

Sprinkle with black pepper and serve piping hot with
crusty bread.

Carrot, Sweet Potato and Ginger Soup

Serves 4–6

Warming and full of goodness, the ginger gives a natural kick and a refreshing flavour to this soup. It is also very soothing for the digestive system, so I'm told!

2 tbsp sunflower oil

2 onions, roughly chopped

500g (1lb 2oz) carrots, roughly sliced

500g (1lb 2oz) sweet potatoes, peeled and roughly chopped

25g (1oz) fresh root ginger, peeled and grated, plus a little extra for garnish

1.5 litres (2½ pints) chicken or vegetable stock

Mary's tips

* *Can be made up to 2 days ahead.*

* *Freezes well.*

Place the oil in a deep saucepan over a high heat. Add the onions and fry for a few minutes. Add the carrots, sweet potatoes and ginger and fry for 3–4 minutes.

Pour in the stock, cover with a lid and bring up to the boil. Reduce the heat and simmer for about 15–20 minutes until the vegetables are tender.

Remove from the heat and season with salt and black pepper. Blend with a hand blender or whiz in a food processor until smooth.

Check the seasoning, sprinkle over some extra grated ginger and serve piping hot with your favourite bread.

For the Love of...Stock

Using homemade stock makes such a huge difference to dishes, it really
is worth the time making some at home. It freezes well, too. There are
a few basic rules to follow and I've listed them here, but you'll find that
with a little bit of effort you'll be rewarded with lots of flavour.

* Never mix raw bones and cooked bones.

* If you don't want to make stock straight away, freeze chicken bones and the
carcass in large poly bags. Once frozen, bash any large bones with a rolling
pin – they break up easily and will then take up less room in the freezer.

* Add flavourings, such as onion, celery, carrots, parsley stalks and bay leaves.

* Don't use green vegetables or leafy herbs, as they will make the stock slimy.

* Don't add starchy vegetables, such as potatoes, as they make the stock cloudy.

* Avoid strongly flavoured root vegetables, such as celeriac
and parsnip, as they may overpower the stock.

* Add onion skins as they will give the stock a lovely colour.

* Season with salt and pepper, but don't overdo it. Remember,
you will be seasoning the dish as well.

* For an intensely flavoured stock, you can reduce it by boiling
rapidly with a lid off, so it is very dark brown.

* Always sieve a stock before using or storing, just in
case there are small splinters of bones.

* Measure the finished stock into empty cream or yoghurt pots in 150ml
(¼ pint), 300ml (½ pint) and 600ml (1 pint) measures; this will help
when making a recipe as the stock will already be measured for use.

* To freeze stock – pour into plastic pots and set aside to cool. Any fat from the stock
will rise to the top and act as a seal, so you won't need a lid. When you come to use it,
remove the fat from the top. If liked, you could use the fat for frying in the recipes.

Vegetable Stock

To make vegetable stock, use veg with lots of flavour, such as carrots, turnips, swede, onions, celery, but not starchy vegetables, such as potatoes and parsnips, as they will make the stock cloudy. Cut the vegetables into chunks and pack tightly into a saucepan with a bay leaf, peppercorns, parsley stalks and the onion skins. Just cover with water, bring to the boil, cover with a lid and simmer for 1–2 hours, until well flavoured. Sieve the liquid away from the veg and store in plastic cartons.

Poultry or Game Stock

After a roast chicken or turkey, use the carcass for stock. Pack the bones tightly into a saucepan and add some vegetables for flavour, such as carrots, turnips, swede and onions cut into chunks (keep the skin on). Cover with water and bring to the boil, then cover with a lid and simmer slowly for 3 hours. Sieve the liquid away from the bones and veg, and store the stock in plastic pots.

If you need chicken stock for a homemade soup and there are no roasted bones available, make stock from raw chicken wings instead. These are relatively inexpensive and any cooked meat can be taken off the bones and added to the soup.

Beef Stock

Ask your butcher for bones for stock and ask him/her to saw any large bones into manageable pieces so they will fit easily into a saucepan. Always brown beef bones ahead in a hot oven. This gives a deeper flavour and a brown colour to the stock. Pack them tightly into a saucepan, add some vegetables for flavour and just cover with water. Bring to the boil, then cover with a lid and simmer for 4–6 hours – the longer the better. Sieve the liquid away from the bones and veg, and store in plastic pots.

FISH

Smoked Haddock Parsley Fishcakes

Makes 8 fishcakes

These are my absolute favourite fishcakes – all the best flavours and
so easy to make. Undyed smoked haddock is off white in colour,
whereas dyed haddock is bright yellow and not so healthy.

500g (1lb 2oz) undyed
   smoked haddock, skin on

A few knobs of butter

500g (1lb 2oz) potatoes,
   peeled and cubed

½ small onion, finely
   chopped

2 tbsp mayonnaise

1 tbsp Dijon mustard

100g (4oz) mature
   Cheddar, grated

2 tbsp chopped parsley

About 75g (3oz) panko
   breadcrumbs

1 tbsp olive oil

....

Mary's tips

* *Can be made up to a day
   ahead and fried to serve.*

* *Freeze well – wrap each
   fishcake individually and
   stack in a container. Can be
   fried straight from frozen
   over a medium heat.*

Preheat the oven to 200°C/180°C fan/Gas 6.

Lay the haddock skin side up on a large piece of buttered
foil. Fold the foil in half over the fish to enclose it and place
on a baking sheet. Bake in the oven for about 15 minutes, or
until the fish is just cooked. The haddock should flake easily
and be lighter in colour. Leave to cool in the foil.

Meanwhile, place the potatoes and onion in a pan of boiling
salted water and cook for about 15 minutes, until tender.
Drain well, return to the pan and mash until smooth. Leave
to cool in a large mixing bowl.

Place the mayonnaise, mustard, cheese, parsley and
25g (1oz) of the panko breadcrumbs into the bowl. Flake
in the fish, discarding the skin, and add 1 tablespoon of the
haddock cooking juices from the foil. Season well and gently
mix with your hands until combined. Shape into
8 fishcakes.

Place the remaining breadcrumbs in a shallow dish and
use to coat the fishcakes. Place them in the freezer for
15 minutes to firm up before cooking.

Heat a little oil and butter in a large frying pan over a
medium heat. Add the fishcakes and fry for 3–4 minutes
on each side, until golden and crisp.

Prawn and Wild Mushroom Stir Fry

Serves 4

Light, healthy and with lovely oriental flavours, this is perfect for sharing with the ones you love. Pak choi is a delicious vegetable; the white bulb stays firm on cooking, giving added texture to the dish, and the green leaves wilt gently.

125g (4½oz) egg noodles or flat rice noodles

2 tbsp sunflower oil

350g (12oz) raw king or tiger prawns, peeled and deveined

1 onion, thinly sliced

6cm (2½in) fresh root ginger, peeled and finely sliced into thin strips

1 garlic clove, crushed

½ red chilli, deseeded and finely sliced

150g (5oz) oyster and/or shiitake mushrooms, sliced

2 pak choi, thinly sliced

3 tbsp hoisin sauce

1 tbsp soy sauce

Juice of ½ small lemon

....

Mary's tips

* *Best made and served.*

* *Not for freezing.*

* *Adding the lemon juice at the last minute really enhances the flavour of the prawns.*

Cook the noodles in a pan of boiling water according to the packet instructions. Drain and run under cold water, then drain again.

Heat 1 tablespoon of the oil in a large frying pan or wok over a high heat. Season the prawns, then add them to the pan and fry quickly until pink. Transfer to a plate.

Heat the remaining oil in the frying pan. Add the onion, ginger, garlic and chilli, and fry for 30 seconds. Add the mushrooms and the pak choi. Stir fry for a few minutes.

Mix the hoisin and soy sauces together in a small bowl, then add to the pan with the cooked noodles. Toss over the heat.

Return the prawns to the pan, add the lemon juice, season well with black pepper and serve at once.

Miso Prawns with Coriander

Serves 4

Japanese miso gives these prawns a wonderful flavour. A fresh-tasting dish, smothered in coriander, these prawns will heighten your senses.

500g (1lb 2oz) raw prawns, peeled and deveined, if necessary

4 large raw king prawns, shell and head on

2 tbsp sunflower oil

Juice of ½ lemon

½ bunch of coriander, chopped

Marinade

1 tbsp white miso paste

1 tbsp soy sauce

1 tbsp runny honey

1 lemongrass stalk, cut into 4 pieces

2 garlic cloves, crushed

1 tbsp sesame oil

1 small red chilli, deseeded and diced

....

Mary's tips

* *Not for freezing.*

* *Can be marinated up to 4 hours ahead.*

Measure all the marinade ingredients into a medium bowl, season with black pepper and whisk together.

Add the prawns and king prawns, and stir to coat well. Transfer to the fridge and leave to marinate for 1 hour, or longer if you have time.

Heat the sunflower oil in a large frying pan or wok over a high heat. Add the shell-on prawns and cook until pink. Turn over and add the rest of the prawns with their marinade and fry for 3–4 minutes, until cooked through, pink and slightly sticky.

Remove the lemongrass, add the lemon juice and coriander, and fry for 1 minute. Give the pan one last toss.

Divide the prawns between four plates, making sure that one unpeeled prawn is on each plate.

Crab Courgetti Spaghetti

Serves 4

I use a handheld spiralizer for the courgettes, but you can buy them
ready-prepared relatively cheaply. They give a lovely texture and
using courgetti means we use less spaghetti in the recipe.

200g (7oz) spaghetti

6 tbsp olive oil

1 large banana shallot,
   thinly sliced

1 red chilli, deseeded
   and diced

2 garlic cloves, crushed

3 courgettes (about
   500g/1lb 2oz), spiralized
   into spaghetti-like strands

100g (4oz) fresh white crab
   meat, or tinned white
   crab meat, drained

Juice of ½ lemon

Small bunch of dill, chopped

....

Mary's tips

* *Best made and served.*
* *Not for freezing.*

Cook the spaghetti in boiling salted water according to the
packet instructions. Drain well.

Place 3 tablespoons of the oil in a large frying pan over a
medium heat. Add the shallot and fry for 3 minutes. Add
the chilli and garlic and fry for 30 seconds. Increase the
heat, add the spiralized courgettes and fry for 2 minutes.
Be careful not to overcook otherwise it will be watery.

Add the crab meat, cooked spaghetti, lemon juice and dill.
Drizzle the remaining oil into the pan and season with salt
and lots of black pepper. Toss everything together then
serve at once.

Crusted Salmon with Samphire and Preserved Lemon Sauce

Serves 4

The semolina on top of the salmon gives a lovely crust and the paprika adds to the flavour and colour. The sauce is bursting with sharpness, and if you wish to preserve your own lemons see page 202 – they are also available from good greengrocers, fish shops and in supermarkets. Samphire is a lovely, salty, green plant that grows naturally by the marshes and on the coast.

25g (1oz) semolina

1 tsp paprika

4 × 125g (4½oz) salmon fillets, skinned

A large knob of soft butter, plus extra for greasing

Small bunch of parsley, stalks removed and reserved

175g (6oz) samphire

½ lemon, cut into 4 wedges, to serve

Lemon Sauce

1 large or 2 small preserved lemons, quartered and pips removed

Juice of ½ lemon

3 tbsp mayonnaise

200g (7oz) crème fraîche

....

Mary's tips

* *Salmon can be prepared with crust on top up to 4 hours ahead. Sauce can be made up to 2 days ahead.*

* *Not for freezing.*

Preheat the oven to 200°C/180°C fan/Gas 6 and butter a baking sheet.

Sprinkle the semolina and paprika on to a large plate and season with salt and black pepper. Spread the top of each salmon fillet with the butter and press the fillets, buttered side down, on to the semolina to give an even crust.

Lay the parsley stalks on the baking sheet and sit the salmon fillets on top of the stalks. Bake in the oven for 15–18 minutes, until the salmon is just opaque and the top is crisp and golden. If liquid is beginning to seep out of the salmon, it is overcooked – it should be holding the juices.

To make the sauce, gather up the parsley leaves and place in a food processor. Add the preserved lemon(s) and whiz until finely chopped. Add the lemon juice, mayonnaise and crème fraîche and season with salt and pepper – go easy on the salt as the lemons are preserved in brine. Process until finely chopped.

When you are ready to serve, boil the samphire in salted water for 2 minutes, then drain, and heat the sauce gently until just melted.

Arrange the hot salmon fillets on a plate with the samphire, sauce and a lemon wedge alongside.

Seared Tuna Steak with Crunchy Coriander and Avocado Salad

Serves 4

So healthy and fresh – tuna is served seared around the edges and
raw in the middle, but if you prefer you can cook it for a little longer.
Be sure to buy sustainable pole- and line-caught tuna.

150g (5oz) French beans,
  sliced into three

½ carrot, peeled into ribbons

1 red pepper, deseeded and
  sliced into thin strips

Bunch of coriander, chopped

1 × 80g packet rocket

2 celery sticks, thinly sliced

100g (4oz) radishes,
  thinly sliced

1 ripe avocado, peeled
  and thinly sliced

3 × 125g (4½oz) raw
  tuna loin steaks

2 tbsp olive oil

Juice of 1 lime

1 tbsp sesame seeds

Dressing

2 tbsp white wine vinegar

1 tbsp soy sauce

1½ tbsp honey

6 tbsp olive oil

½ large garlic clove, crushed

½ large red chilli, deseeded
  and finely chopped

Finely grated zest of 1 lime

....

Mary's tips

* *Not for freezing.*

* *Dressing can be made up to
  a week ahead. Assemble the
  salad up to an hour ahead.*

Measure all the dressing ingredients into a bowl and
whisk until combined. Season with salt and black pepper.

Blanch the French beans in boiling salted water for
3 minutes. Drain, refresh under cold water, then
drain again.

Place the beans, carrot, pepper, coriander, rocket, celery,
radishes and avocado in a serving bowl and toss to mix.

Season the tuna steaks and drizzle with the olive oil.

Heat a non-stick griddle or frying pan until very hot.
Add the tuna steaks and fry for 30 seconds on each side,
until seared on the outside but still pink in the middle.

Remove the tuna from the pan and squeeze over the lime
juice. Slice into thin strips and sprinkle with the sesame seeds.

Serve the tuna with the salad and the dressing poured over
the top.

Salmon and Dill Burger with Lemon Caper Mayonnaise

Makes 8 burgers

Salmon and dill are the perfect combination as the dill gently complements the delicate salmon. Adding the smoked salmon enhances the poached salmon flavour and the topping makes the burger extra special. If you are feeling healthy, just serve as a naked fish burger with no bun.

2½ tbsp sunflower oil

¼ fennel bulb, very thinly sliced

4 brioche buns, split in half and toasted on each side

Salmon Burger

100g (4oz) smoked salmon

500g (1lb 2oz) salmon fillet, skinned and cut into 4cm (1½in) pieces

125g (4½oz) panko breadcrumbs

Juice of ½ lemon

4 tbsp mayonnaise

Small bunch of dill, chopped

Lemon Caper Mayonnaise

4 tbsp mayonnaise

1 tbsp capers, chopped

Juice of ½ small lemon

Topping

4 leaves Romaine lettuce

2 pickled dill cucumbers, thinly sliced

....

Mary's tips

* *Burger can be made up to a day ahead.*

* *Freeze well raw.*

Measure the smoked salmon into a food processor and whiz for a few moments until roughly chopped. Add the remaining burger ingredients and a little salt and black pepper. Whiz again for a moment until the mixture has come together but still has texture. Shape into 8 burgers.

Heat 2 tablespoons of the oil in a large non-stick frying pan over a lowish heat, add the burgers and fry for 3–4 minutes on each side, until golden and cooked through.

Meanwhile, to make the lemon caper mayonnaise, mix all the ingredients together in a small bowl and season well.

Heat the remaining oil in a small pan over high heat and fry the fennel slices for about 5 minutes, until softened and golden.

Place half a lettuce leaf on each bun base and top with a burger, some crispy fennel, slices of dill cucumber and a spoonful of lemon and caper mayonnaise.

Seared Sea Bass Fillet
with Mustard Dill Sauce

Serves 4

My son is a fantastic fisherman and fishing sustainably in our waters is so imperative
– always remember to read the label when buying fish from supermarkets. Sea
bass is a popular fish, good as steak or as fillets, and this sauce is special, too.
We serve it with crispy skin, but if you prefer, remove the skin to serve.

4 sea bass fillets, skin on

Olive oil, to drizzle

Finely grated zest
   of ½ lemon

Mustard Dill Sauce

2 egg yolks

2 tsp plain flour

300ml (½ pint) pouring
   double cream

2 tsp Dijon mustard

1–2 tsp lemon juice

1 tbsp chopped dill

....

Mary's tips

* *Not for freezing.*

* *Sauce can be made up
to a day ahead and
reheated gently to serve.*

Place the sea bass fillets on a board. Drizzle with olive oil
and coat both sides. Sprinkle the flesh side with lemon zest
and season with salt and black pepper.

Heat a large frying pan until hot, then reduce the heat to
very low. Add the sea bass, flesh side down, and seal for
2–3 minutes. When the flesh is sealed, turn the fillets over
on to the skin side and gently cook for 10–12 minutes, until
the skin is crisp and the sea bass is cooked through (this will
depend on the thickness of the fillet).

Meanwhile, to make the sauce, mix the yolks and flour in a
medium bowl. Whisk in the double cream just until smooth.
Transfer to a saucepan and stir over a low to medium heat
until the sauce has thickened. Stir in the mustard, lemon
juice, dill and some seasoning.

Serve the fillet with new potatoes and a green veg, with the
dill sauce drizzled over the top.

Hot Smoked Salmon and Samphire Tart with Parmesan Pastry

Serves 8

Hot smoked salmon comes in packets and is somewhere between smoked salmon and poached salmon with a subtle smokiness to it. The pastry is flavoured with Parmesan, which gives a lovely richness to it.

Pastry

225g (8oz) plain flour

125g (4½oz) butter, cubed

25g (1oz) Parmesan, grated

1 large egg, beaten

About 1 tbsp water

Hot Smoked Salmon Filling

1 tbsp sunflower oil

2 small onions, thinly sliced

150g (5oz) hot smoked salmon fillets, flaked into pieces

Small bunch of dill, chopped

100g (4oz) Gruyère cheese, grated

90g (3½oz) samphire, snipped into small pieces

4 large eggs

300ml (½ pint) double cream

You will need a 28cm (11in) deep, fluted tart tin.

....

Mary's tips

* *Can be made up to 8 hours ahead.*

* *Freezes well cooked.*

To make the pastry, measure the flour, butter and Parmesan into a food processor. Whiz until the mixture resembles fine breadcrumbs. Add the egg and water and whiz again briefly until the mixture comes together to form a dough.

Lightly flour a work surface and roll the pastry out thinly until it is 5cm (2in) bigger than the base of the tin. Carefully lift the pastry and line the tart tin, pressing into the base and sides. Place in the fridge to chill for about 30 minutes.

Preheat the oven to 200°C/180°C fan/Gas 6.

Prick the base, then line with non-stick baking paper and fill with baking beans. Bake for about 15 minutes, then remove the paper and beans and bake for another 5 minutes, until lightly golden. Reduce the oven to 180°C/160°C fan/Gas 4.

Meanwhile, to make the filling, place the oil in a saucepan over a low heat. Add the onions and fry for a few minutes, then cover and cook for about 15 minutes, until soft. Remove the lid and drive off any liquid over a high heat for a minute. Spread the onions over the base of the tart and season with salt and black pepper. Scatter over the salmon pieces, dill, half of the cheese and the samphire.

Mix the eggs and cream together in a jug with a fork to combine. Season with salt and black pepper, then pour over the tart filling. Sprinkle with the remaining cheese and bake for about 30 minutes, until lightly golden and just set in the middle.

Leave to cool for 10 minutes, then remove from the tin and serve warm.

Cod and Crayfish Crumble

Serves 6

Easy to serve all in one dish for the perfect family supper. Crayfish tails can easily be bought from fishmongers or in supermarkets, sometimes in the chilled section. If preferred, you can use the same weight of cooked tiger prawns instead of the crayfish tails.

75g (3oz) butter

1 small onion, thinly sliced

1 small fennel bulb,
   thinly sliced

75g (3oz) plain flour

600ml (1 pint) hot milk

2 tsp Dijon mustard

1 tbsp capers, chopped

2 tbsp chopped parsley

Juice of ½ lemon

50g (2oz) mature
   Cheddar, grated

750g (1¾lb) cod fillet,
   skinned and cut into
   4cm (1½in) cubes

225g (8oz) cooked
   crayfish tails

Topping

200g (7oz) fresh
   breadcrumbs

1 tbsp chopped parsley

100g (4oz) Parmesan, grated

Paprika, to sprinkle

....

Mary's tips

* *Freezes well.*

* *Fish base can be made and chilled up to 6 hours ahead. Top with the crumble topping just before cooking to serve.*

Preheat the oven to 200°C/180°C fan/Gas 6. You will need a deep and wide 1.75 litre (3 pint) ovenproof dish.

Melt the butter in a large saucepan over a high heat. Add the onion and fennel and fry for a few minutes. Lower the heat, cover with a lid and cook for 10 minutes, until soft. Sprinkle in the flour, a little at a time, and stir over the heat for 30 seconds. Gradually pour in the hot milk, whisking until smooth. Add the mustard, capers, parsley, lemon juice and Cheddar and season with salt and black pepper. Stir until melted. Add the cod and crayfish tails and simmer for 2 minutes. Spoon into the ovenproof dish.

To make the topping, measure the breadcrumbs, parsley, Parmesan and seasoning into a bowl and mix. Scatter the topping over the fish mixture and sprinkle with paprika. Bake in the oven for 30–35 minutes, until just bubbling around the edges and golden brown.

Leave to stand for 5 minutes before serving with green vegetables.

POULTRY

Hoisin Chicken with Cashews

Serves 4

This recipe was my go-to in lockdown! Great for a quick supper on a warm summer's evening. Place the chicken breasts in the freezer for an hour or so before you start, so that they are firmer when you cut them into strips.

3 skinless and boneless chicken breasts, cut into long, thin strips

2 tbsp olive oil, plus an extra dash

100g (4oz) cashew nuts

Small bunch of spring onions, sliced

Marinade

3 tbsp hoisin sauce

1 tbsp grated fresh root ginger

1 tsp runny honey

Juice of ½ lemon

....

Mary's tips

* *Best cooked and served.*

* *Marinated chicken freezes well raw.*

To make the marinade, measure the hoisin, ginger, honey and lemon into a bowl. Stir well, then add the chicken strips. Season with salt and pepper, and toss to coat. Cover and place in the fridge to chill for 30 minutes, or longer if possible.

Heat the oil in a large frying pan or wok over a high heat. Fry the chicken for a few minutes in two batches, until golden brown and just cooked through. Remove from the pan and set aside.

Wipe the pan clean with kitchen paper, if needed, then add a dash of oil, the cashew nuts and spring onions and fry for 1 minute.

Return the chicken and juices to the pan and toss over the heat until hot through.

Serve in a bowl with rice or salad on the side.

Chilli Chicken
and Rice Noodle Stir Fry

Serves 4–6

Quick, healthy and bursting with flavour, this is a great dish to teach
teenagers how to make, as they'll enjoy the results. Peas are fine to
add frozen; they will instantly defrost in the hot stir fry.

175g (6oz) thin rice noodles

2 small skinless and
boneless chicken breasts,
sliced into strips

2 tbsp sweet chilli sauce

4 tbsp soy sauce

1 tbsp light muscovado sugar

1 garlic clove, crushed

Juice of 1 lime

2 tbsp sunflower oil

100g (4oz) baby corn, sliced
in half lengthways

1 red onion, finely sliced

1 red chilli, thinly sliced

150g (5oz) sugar snap peas,
destringed, if necessary,
and thinly sliced

75g (3oz) frozen petits pois

Small bunch of
coriander, chopped

75g (3oz) cashew
nuts, chopped

....

Mary's tips

* *Best made and served.*

* *Not for freezing.*

Cook the noodles in a pan of boiling water according to
the packet instructions. Drain, run under cold water, then
drain again.

Season the chicken with salt and black pepper, tip into
a bowl and coat in 1 tablespoon of the sweet chilli sauce.

Mix the remaining chilli sauce with the soy, sugar, garlic
and lime juice in a small bowl.

Place a large frying pan or wok over a high heat until hot.
Add 1 tablespoon of the oil and fry the chicken until golden
and just cooked through. Remove from the pan and set aside.

Add the remaining oil, baby corn, red onion, chilli
and sugar snap peas to the pan. Fry over a high heat for
2 minutes. Add the frozen peas, cooked noodles, coriander,
cooked chicken and the sauce mixture. Toss over the heat
for a few minutes until piping hot. Add the coriander, toss
well and check the seasoning.

Sprinkle with the cashew nuts to serve.

Katsu Chicken

Serves 4

Katsu curry is a Japanese dish, named after the region it is from. Popular in the west, this creamy curry has become a firm favourite in our house.

4 small skinless and boneless chicken breasts

50g (2oz) plain flour

2 eggs, beaten

75g (3oz) panko breadcrumbs

Sunflower oil, for frying

2 spring onions, finely sliced

1 small carrot, finely sliced

Small handful of parsley, roughly chopped

Katsu Sauce

1 tbsp sunflower oil

1 onion, finely chopped

1 celery stick, finely diced

1 small carrot, diced

1 garlic clove, crushed

A small knob of fresh root ginger, peeled and finely grated

2 tbsp curry powder

1 tsp ground turmeric

2 tbsp plain flour

300ml (½ pint) chicken stock

1 × 400g tin full-fat coconut milk

2 tbsp mango chutney

1 tbsp soy sauce

....

Mary's tips

* *Not for freezing.*

* *Sauce can be made up to a day ahead. Chicken can be breaded up to 4 hours ahead.*

To make the sauce, place the oil in a saucepan over a medium heat. Add the onion, celery and carrot and fry for 5 minutes. Add the garlic and ginger and fry for a few seconds. Sprinkle in the curry powder, turmeric and flour, and stir well. Mix in the stock and coconut milk and stir until boiling. Season with salt and black pepper, add the mango chutney and soy, reduce the heat, cover with a lid and simmer for about 10 minutes, until the sauce is coating consistency.

Meanwhile, place the chicken on a board and cover with cling film. Bash with a rolling pin to make them an even thickness. Arrange the flour, egg and breadcrumbs in three separate shallow bowls or deep plates. Season the flour with salt and pepper. Dip each chicken breast first into the flour, then the beaten egg and finally the breadcrumbs, until they are evenly coated.

Place the sunflower oil in a large frying pan over a medium-high heat. Add the chicken breasts and fry for 4–5 minutes on each side, until golden, crisp and cooked through.

Cut each breast into slices and arrange on a plate. Pour over the sauce, garnish with the spring onions, carrot and parsley, and serve with rice.

Warm Five Spice Chicken Salad with Miso Dressing

Serves 4

A wonderful, fresh, crisp and crunchy salad with all the spices and flavours of the orient. To make carrot ribbons, use a vegetable peeler to slice it along the length of the peeled veg.

1 tsp Chinese five
  spice powder

1 tsp honey

1 tbsp olive oil

2 skinless and boneless
  chicken breasts, sliced
  into thin strips

Salad

1 Little Gem lettuce,
  shredded

2 celery sticks, thinly sliced

1 carrot, peeled into ribbons

75g (3oz) radishes, quartered

75g (3oz) beansprouts

1 × 80g packet of pea shoots

75g (3oz) salted cashew nuts

Miso Dressing

2 tsp white miso paste

2 tbsp white wine vinegar

1 tbsp light muscovado sugar

2 tbsp sweet chilli sauce

6 tbsp olive oil

....

Mary's tips

* *Not for freezing.*

* *Dressing can be made
  up to 4 days ahead.
  Assemble salad up to 4
  hours ahead. Add chicken
  and dressing to serve.*

Measure the five spice powder into a small bowl. Add the honey and oil and mix together. Add the chicken, mix well and season with salt and black pepper.

Heat a frying or griddle pan until hot. Add the chicken strips and fry for a few minutes over a high heat, until golden brown and cooked through. Remove from the pan and set aside.

Arrange all the salad ingredients in a serving bowl or platter.

Mix the dressing ingredients together in a small jug.

Scatter the warm chicken on top of the salad and drizzle over the dressing just before serving.

Kashmiri Chicken Curry

Serves 6

This is a hot and spicy curry, rich in flavour. If you want it to be more mellow, leave out the red chilli. It seems a lot of ingredients, but most are spices, which you will hopefully already have in your spice cupboard. They are all needed for the authenticity of the curry.

Spice Mix

1 tbsp medium curry powder

1 tbsp ground cinnamon

1 tbsp ground cumin

1 tbsp ground coriander

1 tbsp paprika

2 tsp ground turmeric

2 tsp ground allspice

Curry

8 chicken thighs, bone in and skin on

2 tbsp sunflower oil

2 onions, roughly chopped

1 red pepper, deseeded and diced

A large knob of fresh root ginger, peeled and grated

3 garlic cloves, crushed

2 red chillies, deseeded and diced

2 tbsp plain flour

450ml (¾ pint) chicken stock

Finely grated zest and juice of 1 lime

1 large sweet potato, peeled and cubed

Small bunch of coriander, chopped

....

Mary's tips

* *Can be made up to 2 days ahead and reheated.*

* *Freezes well.*

Combine all the ingredients for the spice mix in a small bowl and mix well.

Place the chicken thighs in a large bowl, add 2 tablespoons of the spice mix and turn to coat well. Cover and place in the fridge to marinate for a few hours or overnight. Keep the remaining spice mix to add later.

Preheat the oven to 160°C/140°C fan/Gas 3.

Heat the oil in a deep ovenproof frying pan or shallow flameproof casserole over a high heat. Add the chicken and fry for a few minutes, until brown on all sides. Remove from the dish and set aside.

Add the onions and pepper to the dish and fry for a few minutes. Stir in the ginger, garlic and chillies and fry for a few seconds. Sprinkle in the remaining spice mix and the flour and fry for a few seconds.

Pour in the stock, lime zest and juice, and stir well until combined. Bring up to the boil and return the chicken to the dish. Cover with a lid and transfer to the oven for 30 minutes.

Add the sweet potato and return to the oven for another 30 minutes, or until the chicken and sweet potatoes are cooked through.

Season well with salt and pepper and add the coriander just before serving with pilau rice (see page 169), poppadoms and naan bread.

One Pot Chicken
with Pearl Barley and Thyme

Serves 6

All cooked in one pot, this healthy chicken and pearl barley dish is a great one
to feed a gang and is high in fibre, too. Serve with green vegetables.

1 tbsp sunflower oil

8 skinless chicken
   thighs, bone in

1 large onion, chopped

2 carrots, finely diced

2 large garlic cloves, crushed

225g (8oz) pearl barley

200ml (⅓ pint) white wine

700ml (1¼ pints)
   chicken stock

3 sprigs of thyme

125g (4½oz) frozen
   petits pois

Juice of ½ lemon

Small bunch of
   parsley, chopped

....

Mary's tips

* *Best made and served.*

* *Not for freezing.*

* *Use as wide-based a pan
as possible, so the liquid
can reduce. If you use a
small pan, you may have
a little excess liquid at the
end of the cooking time.*

Preheat the oven to 150°C/130°C fan/Gas 2.

Place the oil in a wide-based ovenproof frying pan or
flameproof casserole over a high heat. Season the chicken
thighs and brown them on all sides, until golden. Remove
from the dish and set aside.

Add the onion and carrots to the dish and fry for a few
minutes. Add the garlic and fry for 30 seconds. Stir in the
pearl barley and pour in the wine. Bring to the boil and
allow the wine to reduce for a few seconds. Add the stock
and thyme sprigs, cover with a lid and boil for 10 minutes.

Return the chicken to the pan, transfer the dish, uncovered,
to the oven and cook for about 50–60 minutes, until the
pearl barley is tender. Stir in the petits pois and lemon juice
for the final 5 minutes of the cooking time.

Remove the sprigs of thyme, sprinkle with the chopped
parsley and serve hot.

Spanish Chicken and Chickpea Stew

Serves 4–6

Full of Mediterranean flavours, this is a hearty dish. Serve in a deep
bowl with a chunk of bread – perfect for chilly days. The sauce is
fairly thin and would also go well with mashed potato or rice.

2 tbsp olive oil

8 skinless chicken
   thighs, bone in

2 large onions, sliced

2 celery sticks, thinly sliced

2 garlic cloves, crushed

1 tbsp paprika

150ml (¼ pint) sherry

300ml (½ pint) chicken stock

1 × 400g tin chopped
   tomatoes

1 tbsp tomato purée

100g (4oz) pitted black olives

1 × 400g tin chickpeas,
   drained and rinsed

1 tbsp chopped sage

....

Mary's tips

* *Can be made up to
  a day ahead.*

* *Freezes well.*

Heat the oil in a large, deep frying pan or flameproof
casserole over a high heat. Season the chicken thighs with
salt and black pepper, then add to the pan and fry until
brown on all sides. Remove from the pan and set aside.

Add the onions and celery to the pan and fry for 3–4 minutes.
Stir in the garlic and paprika and fry for another 30 seconds.

Pour in the sherry and stock and tip in the tin of tomatoes.
Stir in the purée and bring up to the boil. Add the chicken
thighs, olives, chickpeas and sage and season well. Cover
and bring back to the boil, then reduce the heat and simmer
for 30 minutes.

Remove the lid and continue to simmer for about 15 minutes
on the hob, or until the chicken is cooked through and the
sauce has reduced a little.

Check the seasoning and serve piping hot with green veg
and crusty bread.

For the Love of...Herbs

I have always been passionate about growing herbs, as I'm not keen on using dried, though I sometimes use dried dill to make gravadlax. Even when I was younger and lived in a flat in London, I would grow basil, parsley and chives in small pots on the windowsill, so they could grow towards the light. Keep snipping and they will come back time and time again.

Basil

A green-leaf herb, there are many different types available – Thai, lemon and lime, for example. I like the classic, large-leafed, sweet basil best. It grows well in the summer months in a sunny place. Break off the leaves, chop and add at the last minute to dishes. Perfect for pesto, with mozzarella, vine tomatoes and other Mediterranean dishes.

Chives

From the onion family, you can buy plain or garlic chives. They have a lovely purple flower in the height of summer, so snip these off and use them as a decoration for salads. Common chives have a long, tubular leaf, while garlic chives are flatter. It is best to cut them using scissors, as they are tricky to chop with a knife. Keep them well-watered if you are growing them in a pot. Cut a bundle, tie with a piece of string, wrap in foil, then freeze. Snip from frozen and any unused chives can be returned to the freezer.

Bay

Bay leaves have an intense flavour and are used purely for infusing. Add whole leaves to a stew or soup and remove them at the end of cooking. They are also good with a slice of cucumber in a gin and tonic! Bay is a hardy leaf so not appropriate for chopping. Grown in pots, it is an attractive all-year-round plant.

Dill

Dill is perfect with fish. I grow it at home in old wooden wine boxes and cut it regularly – it likes to grow in a controlled space. Dill is dark green and is not to be confused with fennel, which has wispy fronds and a strong aniseed flavour.

Lemongrass

A wonderful oriental bulb that is best bought in stems. It takes a while to tenderise, so best to bash the stems with a rolling pin (to break up the fibres) and add them whole to a dish or sauce. Allow the flavour to infuse, then discard the stem before serving.

Rosemary

This hardy, evergreen shrub can be grown with vegetables or in the flower bed. The spiky leaves need chopping finely when adding to stews, or use sprigs when roasting lamb.

Tarragon

Only buy or grow French tarragon, rather than Russian, which has no flavour. French tarragon has soft, long leaves which chop easily and have a faint aniseed taste. The flavour marries perfectly with chicken and fish.

Mint

A wonderful perennial herb, there are many different varieties and flavours of mint, and with differently shaped leaves, too. I grow the plain, pointed-leaf variety as it is great for cooking, infusing in tea and the small tender leaves are good for decoration, as well. Some mints, such as spearmint, can be quite overpowering, so choose carefully.

Thyme

An aromatic, small-leafed herb, there are many different varieties and flavours of thyme. I like to use thyme sprigs in a casserole – at the end of cooking, the leaves will have fallen off so you just have to remove the stems. The flavour is a wonderful match with fish, meat and lemon.

Parsley

Available as flat-leaf or curly English parsley, I prefer flat-leaf, which is tender and some people say has more flavour – I find them both the same! The leaves are best chopped and used at the end of cooking, while the stalks can be added early for flavour.

Herbed Marinated Chicken

Serves 6

Using chicken legs for this recipe gives maximum flavour. These would also be great cooked on a BBQ. The legs are boned so save the bones for making stock. If you buy your chicken from a butcher, you can ask them to remove the bones for you. I always try to support my local butchers – it would be so sad to see them leave our high streets. The local suppliers and traders are the beating heart of our villages and towns, and we must support them when we can. Their knowledge is irreplaceable, too.

6 chicken legs

2 tbsp olive oil

2 large garlic cloves, crushed

2 tbsp chopped fresh mint

1 tbsp chopped
   fresh tarragon

2 tbsp chopped fresh thyme

Finely grated zest and
   juice of 1 lemon

2 tbsp runny honey

....

Mary's tips

* *Can be marinated up
 to a day ahead.*

* *The marinated chicken
 freezes well raw.*

Place the chicken legs on a board. Using a sharp knife, slice the thigh meat either side of the thigh bone to remove the bone. Tunnel bone around the joint down to the drumstick and pull the bone through, or cut through the meat to remove the bone.

Mix the olive oil, garlic, herbs and lemon zest and juice in a large bowl. Add the chicken legs and turn to coat in the marinade. Cover and place in the fridge to marinate for at least 2 hours, or ideally overnight.

Preheat the oven to 220°C/200°C fan/Gas 7.

Arrange the chicken legs, tucked into a ball, rounded side up, in a single layer in a small roasting tin and season well with salt and black pepper. Drizzle over the honey. Roast for 30–35 minutes until the chicken is cooked through and the skin crispy and golden.

Serve hot or cold with the cooking juices drizzled on top.

Chilled Herb Pesto Chicken

Serves 6

Perfect for a summer lunch and feeding a gang, it's better to prepare this ahead so that the herbs infuse into the chicken. Full-fat British yoghurt is available in good supermarkets; it is thick, rich and creamy – Greek yoghurt is the same.

4 celery sticks, sliced

1.2kg (2lb 10oz) whole chicken, cooked, meat removed from the carcass and torn into strips

200g (7oz) full-fat natural yoghurt

100g (4oz) mayonnaise

1 Romaine lettuce, shredded

2 tbsp pine nuts, toasted

Herb Dressing

2 tbsp Dijon mustard

2 tbsp white wine vinegar

4 tbsp olive oil

4 tbsp fresh basil pesto

1 banana shallot, finely sliced

1 fat garlic clove, crushed

1 tsp caster sugar

Small bunch each of tarragon, dill and basil, chopped

Juice of ½ lemon

....

Mary's tips

* *Not for freezing.*

* *Chicken can be dressed up to a day ahead. Mix with the yoghurt and mayonnaise up to 8 hours ahead.*

To make the dressing, measure the mustard, vinegar, oil and pesto into a large bowl. Whisk until it comes together. Add the shallot, garlic, sugar, herbs and lemon, mix well and season with salt and black pepper.

Add the celery and chicken to the dressing and mix to coat well. Cover and place in the fridge to chill for 4–6 hours or overnight.

Measure the yoghurt and mayonnaise into a large bowl. Add the chicken mixture, check the seasoning and stir to combine. Taste and add more herbs or seasoning, if you like.

Arrange the lettuce on the base of a platter and spoon the chicken salad on top. Scatter with the toasted pine nuts to serve.

Rather Special Chicken
and Herb Casserole

Serves 4–6

An all-in-one dish to cook and serve. Sage was often used as a dried herb
in recipes but now it is readily available fresh and is simple to grow. It
comes with either green or purple leaves – they both taste the same.

250g (9oz) dry cured bacon,
snipped into small pieces

2 large onions, chopped

8 skinless chicken
thighs, bone in

2 tbsp sunflower oil

30g (1¼oz) plain flour

150ml (¼ pint) hot
chicken stock

150ml (¼ pint) dry
white wine

2 large sprigs of thyme

Small bunch of sage, 6 leaves
removed for garnish

2 bay leaves

200g (7oz) small chestnut
mushrooms, quartered

100g (4oz) full-fat
crème fraîche

A knob of butter

Small bunch of
parsley, chopped

Mary's tips

* *Can be made up to a day
  ahead. Add the crème
  fraîche and mushrooms
  when reheating.*

* *Freezes well.*

Preheat the oven to 160°C/140°C fan/Gas 3.

Place the bacon in a large non-stick ovenproof frying pan or
flameproof casserole and fry over a medium heat for a few
minutes to render out the fat. Add the onions and continue to
fry until the bacon is brown at the edges. Transfer the bacon
and onions to a plate using a slotted spoon and set aside.

Lightly season the chicken. Place the oil in the unwashed
dish, add the chicken and brown over a high heat, turning
once. Transfer to the plate with the bacon and onions.

Scatter the flour into the dish (adding a little more oil, if
needed) and stir to combine. Gradually incorporate the hot
stock, whisking, and allow to thicken. Pour in the wine and
return the bacon, onions and chicken to the pan. Stir well,
add the thyme sprigs, sage sprigs and bay leaves. The sauce
will be quite thick at this stage. Bring to the boil, season
well with salt and black pepper and cover. Transfer to the
oven for 30 minutes.

Remove the dish from the oven and add the mushrooms and
crème fraîche. Stir well and return to the oven for a further
15–20 minutes, until the chicken is tender.

Meanwhile, heat the butter in a small pan over a medium
heat. Add the whole sage leaves and fry until crisp.

Remove the bay leaves, thyme and sage sprigs from the
casserole and discard (some leaves will have fallen off to
flavour the casserole). Stir in the parsley and serve with the
crisp sage leaves on top.

Chicken, Spinach and Blue Cheese Risotto

Serves 4–6

Rich and creamy in texture and flavour, risottos need care and love to make and should not be rushed. Dolcelatte is a salted blue cheese, so go easy on the salt when seasoning.

350g (12oz) skinless and boneless chicken thighs

1 litre (1¾ pints) chicken stock

1 bay leaf

2 tbsp olive oil

A knob of butter

1 large onion, chopped

3 garlic cloves, crushed

225g (8oz) risotto rice

150ml (¼ pint) white wine

225g (8oz) peeled butternut squash, cut into 1cm (½ in) pieces

100g (4oz) baby spinach, roughly chopped

100g (4oz) Dolcelatte cheese, cubed

Squeeze of lemon juice

....

Mary's tips

* *Poaching the chicken keeps it tender and the stock adds flavour to the risotto, too.*
* *Best made and served.*
* *Not for freezing.*

Place the chicken thighs in a saucepan with the stock and bay leaf. Cover with a lid and bring to the boil. After a couple of minutes, lower the heat and simmer very gently for 15–20 minutes, or until the thighs are poached and cooked through.

Remove the chicken with a slotted spoon and slice into bite-size pieces. You should have just over 1 litre (1¾ pints) chicken stock left in the pan. Remove the bay leaf and return the stock to a low heat.

Place 1 tablespoon of the oil and the knob of butter in a deep frying pan over a high heat. Add the onion and garlic and fry for a few minutes. Add the rice and stir to coat in the oil. Pour in the wine and allow to reduce over a high heat for a few minutes.

Reduce the heat and add the hot stock, a ladleful at a time, stirring occasionally, until most of the liquid has been absorbed and the rice is nearly cooked. This will take about 20 minutes.

Meanwhile, place the remaining oil in a small frying pan over a medium heat. Add the squash and fry for 8–10 minutes, until cooked.

When the risotto is nearly cooked, add the spinach and stir until wilted. Add the chicken pieces, cooked squash and Dolcelatte cheese and gently fold everything together. Add a little more stock if the risotto is too thick. Season well with salt and black pepper, squeeze over the lemon juice and serve at once.

Coconut Ginger Chicken

Serves 4

The perfect dish for when you have friends over for supper. It is full of flavour and quick to make – this should be your go-to recipe. Lemongrass takes a long time to tenderise so bash the stalks with a wooden rolling pin to split the stems. If you like spicy food, add more chilli!

4 small skinless and
  boneless chicken breasts

2 tsp runny honey

3 tbsp sunflower oil

2 lemongrass stalks, bashed

Small bunch of Thai basil,
  chopped, stalks reserved

Finely grated zest and
  juice of 1 lime

1 large onion, finely chopped

6cm (2½in) fresh root ginger,
  peeled and finely grated

½ red chilli, deseeded
  and diced

1 × 400g tin full-fat
  coconut milk

1 tsp fish sauce

1 tsp light muscovado sugar

3 tbsp chopped coriander

Mary's tips

* *Not for freezing.*

* *Sauce can be made up
to a day ahead. Add the
lemongrass stalk from
roasting the chicken to the
sauce when reheating.*

Preheat the oven to 200°C/180°C fan/Gas 6 and line a small roasting tin with non-stick baking paper.

Place the chicken breasts on a board, season with salt and black pepper and spread the honey over them.

Heat 2 tablespoons of the oil in a large frying pan over a high heat. Add the chicken breasts and brown on just one side until golden. Remove from the heat.

Arrange one of the stalks of lemongrass and the basil stalks in a pile in the small roasting tin and sit the chicken breasts on top, brown side up. Drizzle half the lime juice over the top and roast for about 15 minutes, or until just cooked through. Remove from the oven, cover and leave to rest.

Meanwhile, place the remaining oil in the frying pan. Add the onion and fry over a high heat for a few minutes, then cover with a lid, lower the heat and cook for about 10 minutes until soft.

Increase the heat, add the ginger and chilli and fry for a few seconds. Whisk in the coconut milk, then add the remaining lemongrass, the fish sauce and sugar, and stir. Cover with a lid, reduce the heat and simmer for about 5 minutes, adding any juices from the resting chicken.

Remove the lemongrass from the sauce and add the grated zest and remaining lime juice, the coriander and Thai basil. Check the seasoning, then spoon a little sauce on each plate.

Carve the chicken into slices and arrange on top of the sauce. Serve with rice, a green veg and the remaining sauce on the side.

Pan Fried Duck Breast
Noodle Stir Fry

Serves 6

This quick and healthy stir fry is a great and different way to serve duck breasts. Noodles can be bought in different thicknesses; we prefer the fine ones, but you can use any you like.

2 duck breasts

175g (6oz) fine egg noodles

Small bunch of spring onions, sliced

1 red pepper, deseeded and thinly sliced

200g (7oz) mixed mushrooms (such as shiitake and chestnut), sliced

Small bunch of coriander, chopped

Marinade

6 tbsp hoisin sauce

2 tbsp soy sauce

2cm (¾ in) fresh root ginger, peeled and finely grated

1 garlic clove, crushed

Juice of 1 lemon

1 red chilli, deseeded and diced

Mary's tips

* *Prepare ahead and cook to serve.*

* *Raw marinated duck breast freezes well.*

* *It is easier to cut the duck into thin slices if you cut them when they are slightly frozen.*

To make the marinade, measure all the ingredients into a small bowl and mix.

Remove the skin from the duck breasts and slice the skin into very thin strips with scissors. Slice each duck breast widthways into 6–8 pieces. Transfer the duck breast pieces to a bowl and add 2 tablespoons of the marinade. Toss to coat and season with salt and black pepper. Leave to marinate for 30 minutes.

Cook the noodles in a pan of boiling salted water according to the packet instructions. Drain, run under cold water, then drain again.

Meanwhile, place a large non-stick frying pan or wok over a high heat. Add the strips of duck skin and fry until crispy and brown. Remove to a plate using a slotted spoon. Carefully pour all but 1 tablespoon of the duck fat into a small bowl to use later (this will have rendered out of the skin). Add the duck breast pieces to the pan without the marinade and fry over a high heat for 2 minutes, turning to brown on all sides, then transfer to a plate to rest.

Add a tablespoon of the reserved duck fat to the pan, then add the spring onions, pepper and mushrooms and fry for about 3 minutes, so they still hold their shape. Add the noodles and reserved marinade and toss for a few minutes until heated through. Check the seasoning, add the chopped coriander, toss again, then turn the noodles out on to a serving platter. Arrange the duck breasts on top and scatter over the crispy duck skin to serve.

Roasted Duck Legs Japanese Style

Serves 6

These have been inspired by our daughter Annabel's love of Japanese cooking. On her travels, she took a day's cooking course in Kyoto and learnt authentic methods and flavours. As a nation we have embraced the fresh, full-flavoured cuisine and, for me, duck is the perfect recipe to show it off.

6 duck legs (about 250g/9oz each)

900ml (1½ pints) chicken stock

6cm (2½in) fresh root ginger, peeled and cut into 8

2 fat garlic cloves, each quartered

Sauce

2 tsp cornflour

6 tbsp white miso paste

4 tbsp soy sauce

Finely grated zest and juice of 1 lime

5cm (2in) fresh root ginger, peeled and very finely grated

2 tbsp sesame oil

6 tbsp maple syrup

3 tbsp Japanese rice vinegar or white wine vinegar

2 tbsp pomegranate molasses

....

Mary's tips

* *Duck legs can be poached up to a day ahead. Sauce can be made up to 4 days ahead.*

* *Freezes well after first cooking.*

To make the sauce, measure the cornflour into a small pan and stir in the miso paste, soy, lime zest and juice until smooth. Add the remaining ingredients and a little salt and black pepper. Bring to the boil, stirring all the time, until thickened and coating the spoon. Set aside.

To cook the duck, arrange the legs in a large saucepan so they fit snugly in a single layer. Cover with the stock and add the ginger and garlic. Bring to the boil, cover, reduce the heat and simmer for about 1½ hours, or until tender. Set aside to cool in the stock.

Preheat the oven 220°C/200°C fan/Gas 7.

Remove the duck legs from the cooking liquid, reserving a small amount for the sauce, and place the legs in a single layer, skin side up, in a roasting tin. Brush a little of the sauce over the top of the duck legs and slide into the oven for about 20–25 minutes, until glazed and brown.

Meanwhile, reheat the remaining sauce in a small pan. Add a little of the reserved stock to thin the sauce, if necessary, then serve alongside the legs with pak choi or edamame beans.

PORK, BEEF
AND LAMB

Spanish Hot Pot

Serves 6

Cooked in one pot on the hob, the chorizo and paprika give a smoky flavour to this dish and a deep, rich colour, too. Serve it on its own or with rice, mash or crusty bread.

500g (1lb 2oz) pork fillet, sliced into thin strips

1 tbsp honey

2 tbsp olive oil

150g (5oz) chorizo, diced

1 large onion, chopped

1 red pepper, deseeded and diced

1 yellow pepper, deseeded and diced

2 garlic cloves, crushed

2 tsp paprika

2 tbsp plain flour

2 tbsp tomato purée

Pinch of saffron

1 × 400g tin chopped tomatoes

300ml (½ pint) chicken stock

2 bay leaves

2 tbsp chopped parsley

Mary's tips

* *Can be made up to 8 hours ahead and reheated.*

* *Freezes well.*

Place the pork in a bowl and drizzle the honey over the top. Turn to coat and season with salt and black pepper.

Heat the oil in a deep frying pan or flameproof casserole over a high heat. Add the pork and fry quickly until browned. Remove from the pan with a slotted spoon and set aside.

If the pan is dark, wipe it clean and add a little more oil before adding the chorizo. Fry for 3 minutes until crisp. Add the onion, peppers and garlic and fry for a few more minutes. Sprinkle in the paprika and flour, and stir in the tomato purée and saffron. Stir in the chopped tomatoes and stock, stirring, and bring to the boil. Season and add the bay leaves. Cover with a lid, reduce the heat and simmer for about 20 minutes.

Return the pork to the pan and simmer for a further 5 minutes.

Remove the bay leaves and stir in the chopped parsley to serve.

Sausage Spinach Filo Swirl

Serves 6

There are not many ingredients and it is so simple to make but so very
tasty to eat! Similar to Greek spanakopita using filo pastry and spinach,
I bake it in a cake tin to help the sausage swirl keep its shape.

A knob of butter

1 small leek, finely chopped

1 garlic clove, crushed

150g (5oz) baby spinach

6 of your favourite pork
sausages (500g/1lb
2oz total weight)

4 sheets of filo pastry
(each sheet 25 ×
45cm/10 × 18in)

50g (2oz) butter, melted

1 tbsp sesame seeds

. . . .

Mary's tips

* *Can be prepared ready
for baking up to 8 hours
ahead, then cooked to serve.
It can be cooked up to 4
hours ahead and reheated
in a hot oven to serve.*

* *Freezes well raw.*

Preheat the oven to 220°C/200°C fan/Gas 7. Grease the
sides of a 20cm (8in) loose-bottomed cake tin and place the
ring on a baking sheet (no need to use the base of the tin).

Melt the knob of butter in a saucepan over a high heat.
Add the leek and fry for a few minutes, then cover with
a lid, lower the heat and cook for about 10 minutes, or
until soft.

Increase the heat, add the garlic and spinach and fry for few
minutes, until the spinach has wilted. Tip all the vegetables
into a bowl to cool.

Remove the sausage meat from their skins and place in the
bowl with the cooled leeks and spinach. Season with black
pepper and mix using your hands.

Brush the sheets of filo with the melted butter and stick
them together end to end in two layers to make a long
rectangle measuring about 25 × 90cm (10 × 36in).

Shape the sausage mixture into a long sausage, the same
length as the filo. Place it along one long edge of the pastry
and roll, brushing with butter in between each roll. You
should end up with a long sausage encased in filo. Bend
the filo roll into the ring to make a swirl. Brush the top
with more butter and sprinkle with the sesame seeds.
Place on the hot baking sheet and cook in the oven for
40–45 minutes, until golden and crisp.

Remove the ring and cut into wedges to serve.

Sweet and Sour Pork

Serves 4–6

Often a favourite with the young – the pork is lightly coated to give a
puffed-up texture and although chunks of pineapple were traditionally
added to the dish, I am not so keen; the pineapple juice is enough for me!
I use juice from a carton and save the remainder for breakfast.

1 egg white

15g (½oz) cornflour

1 large pork fillet
(about 350g/12oz),
sliced into strips

2 tbsp sunflower oil

1 onion, finely sliced

2 carrots, finely sliced

1 red pepper, deseeded
and sliced

A large knob of fresh root
ginger, peeled and grated

6 spring onions, trimmed
and finely sliced

Sweet and Sour Sauce

1 tsp cornflour

150ml (¼ pint)
pineapple juice

3 tbsp soy sauce

1 tbsp light muscovado sugar

2 tbsp vinegar

1 tbsp ketchup

2 tbsp honey

Mary's tips

* *Can be prepared up to
4 hours ahead, but
best cooked to serve.*

* *Not for freezing.*

Mix the egg white and cornflour together in a bowl. Season
the pork with salt and black pepper then add to the bowl
and mix to coat in the cornflour mixture. Leave to marinate
for 30 minutes.

To make the sauce, measure the cornflour into a bowl and
add the pineapple juice. Stir gently until smooth. Add the
remaining sauce ingredients and mix well.

Heat the oil in a large frying pan or wok over a high heat.
Add the pork and fry until golden on all sides and just
cooked through. Take care not to overcook as that would
make the pork tough. Remove the pork with a slotted spoon
and set aside.

Add the onion, carrots and pepper to the pan and fry for
3–5 minutes. Stir in the ginger and return the pork to the
pan. Pour in the sauce and bring up to the boil, stirring.
Reduce the heat and simmer for about 2 minutes.

Add the spring onions, check the seasoning and serve piping
hot with rice.

Pancetta and Tenderstem Broccoli Carbonara

Serves 4–6

This has a lot of sauce so if you are feeding a gang, you can add up
to 300g (10½ oz) pasta and reduce the broccoli, if you like. Pecorino
is a salty cheese and not quite as creamy as Parmesan.

400g (14oz) tenderstem
broccoli

225g (8oz) linguine

1 tbsp olive oil

250g (9oz) pancetta, diced

1 garlic clove, crushed

3 large eggs

150g (5oz) pecorino
cheese, finely grated

....

Mary's tips

* *Not for freezing.*

* *Pasta and broccoli can
be cooked an hour ahead,
refreshed in cold water to
stop the cooking and drained
before adding to the sauce.*

Cut the top florets from the broccoli and slice the stems.

Cook the pasta in boiling salted water according to the
packet instructions, adding the broccoli for the last
3 minutes of the cooking time. Drain and reserve 150ml
(¼ pint) of the pasta water in a small jug.

Meanwhile, place the oil in a large frying pan over a medium
heat. Add the pancetta and fry for a few minutes, until crispy.

Drain away any excess fat, then add the garlic and fry for a
few seconds.

Beat the eggs and cheese together in a bowl.

Add the pasta and broccoli to the frying pan with the
reserved cooking water and mix for a few seconds. Remove
the pan from the heat, add the egg mixture and toss until
the sauce coats everything well. Season well with black
pepper and a little salt and serve at once.

Sticky Soy and Ginger Pork Fillet

Serves 4

Roasting a whole fillet is so quick to do and this delicious marinade makes
it easy and full of flavour. There is enough marinade here for a sauce, too.
Make sure you heat it well before pouring over the cooked pork.

1 large pork fillet
(600g/1lb 6oz)

4 spring onions, finely
shredded into long,
thin strips

1 red chilli, deseeded
and thinly sliced

2 tbsp chopped coriander

Marinade

4cm (1½in) fresh root
ginger, peeled and grated

2 garlic cloves, crushed

4 tbsp soy sauce

2 tbsp sweet chilli sauce

3 tbsp honey

Mary's tips

* *Can be marinated up to
8 hours ahead. If serving
cold can be roasted up
to 4 hours ahead.*

* *Freezes well raw in
the marinade.*

To make the marinade, measure all the ingredients into
a dish and mix well.

Trim any sinew from the fillet and discard. Sit the fillet in
the marinade, season with salt and black pepper and turn
to coat until all the fillet is covered. Leave to marinate for
a few hours in the fridge.

Preheat the oven to 220°C/200°C fan/Gas 7 and line a small
roasting tin with non-stick baking paper.

Removed the fillet from the marinade (reserving the
marinade to use later) and sit it in the roasting tin. Roast
in the oven for 25–30 minutes, until golden brown and
cooked through.

Remove the fillet from the roasting tin and set aside on
a board to rest. Cover with foil and leave for 5 minutes
before carving.

Place the reserved marinade in a small saucepan and
place over a medium heat. Bring to a simmer, stirring
occasionally.

Carve the pork into slices and arrange on a platter. Pour
the hot marinade over the top and scatter with the spring
onions, red chilli and coriander. Serve with rice or noodles.

Pork and Apple Burger

Makes 6 burgers

Something a bit different, topped with apple sauce and crispy bacon; these
are wonderful pork burgers. If you've served pulled pork for Sunday lunch,
you could use any leftovers in a burger instead and top with BBQ sauce.

1 tbsp sunflower oil

6 brioche buns, split in half

Burger

1 dessert apple, peeled,
    cored and diced

1 onion, finely chopped

1 tbsp chopped sage

1 tbsp chopped parsley

Finely grated zest
    of ½ lemon

500g (1lb 2oz) minced pork

75g (3oz) fresh breadcrumbs

Topping

6 tbsp apple sauce

6 rashers of bacon, fried
    until crispy, and halved

Measure all the burger ingredients together into a bowl,
season with salt and black pepper. Mix until combined
using your hands. Shape into 6 burgers.

Heat the oil in a large frying pan over a high heat. Add the
burgers and fry for 5 minutes on each side, until cooked
through and golden.

Place each burger in a bun and top with a tablespoon of
apple sauce and two pieces of crispy bacon.

Mary's tips

* *Burgers can be made up
    to 12 hours ahead and
    kept in the fridge.*

* *Freeze well raw.*

Loaded Chilli Combo Burger

Makes 6 burgers

This is just for the brave – chilli-infused and with extra jalapeños
on top. Lucy's husband, Pedro, loves this one!

1 tbsp sunflower oil
6 brioche buns, split in half

Burger

1 onion, finely chopped
250g (9oz) minced beef
250g (9oz) minced pork
1 red chilli, deseeded
   and finely chopped
2 garlic cloves, crushed
Dash of tabasco or
   chilli sauce
1 tbsp chopped parsley
75g (3oz) fresh breadcrumbs

Topping

3 tbsp mayonnaise
1 tbsp jalapeño peppers
2 tbsp tomato salsa
6 slices mozzarella
1 avocado, peeled and sliced
1 Romaine lettuce, shredded

Mary's tips

* Burgers can be made up
  to 12 hours ahead and
  kept in the fridge.
* Freeze well raw.

Measure all the burger ingredients into a bowl, season with
salt and black pepper and mix until combined using your
hands. Shape into 6 burgers.

Heat the oil in a large frying pan over a high heat. Add
the burgers and fry for about 5 minutes on each side until
cooked through.

Place each burger in a brioche bun and top with some
mayonnaise, jalapeño peppers, salsa, a slice of mozzarella
cheese, avocado and some lettuce.

Pork and Apple　　　　　**Loaded Chilli Combo**

Beef and Horseradish Mustard

Minted Lamb with Feta

Beef and Horseradish Mustard Burger

Makes 6 burgers

The horseradish and mustard give these burgers a comforting heat and deep flavour. If you are cooking the burgers in batches, fry them over a medium heat.

1 tbsp sunflower oil
6 brioche buns, split in half

Burger
1 large onion, finely chopped
500g (1lb 2oz) minced beef
1 tbsp creamed hot horseradish
1 tbsp Dijon mustard
1 tbsp chopped fresh thyme
75g (3oz) fresh breadcrumbs

Topping
A little creamed hot horseradish, Dijon mustard and mayonnaise
1 Little Gem lettuce
2 gherkins, sliced

Mary's tips

* *Burgers can be made up to 12 hours ahead and kept in the fridge.*
* *Freeze well raw.*

Measure all the burger ingredients into a bowl. Season with salt and black pepper and mix until combined using your hands. Shape into 6 burgers.

Heat the oil in a large frying pan over a high heat. Add the burgers and fry for about 4 minutes on each side, until cooked through.

Place each burger in a brioche bun and top with horseradish, mustard, mayonnaise, lettuce and slices of gherkin.

Minted Lamb Burger with Feta

Makes 6 burgers

The combination of freshly chopped mint and bought mint from a jar gives
the burgers the best mint flavour. Even when I serve roast lamb, I make a fresh
mint sauce using home-grown mint and add a little sauce from a jar.

1 tbsp sunflower oil

6 brioche buns, split in half

Burger

1 garlic clove, crushed

1 large onion, finely chopped

500g (1lb 2oz) lean
   minced lamb

75g (3oz) fresh breadcrumbs

1 tbsp mint sauce from a jar

5 tbsp chopped fresh mint

Topping

3 tsp mint sauce from a
   jar, plus extra to serve

3 tsp mayonnaise

2 dill cucumbers, sliced

6 thin slices feta cheese

Handful of rocket leaves

....

Mary's tips

* *Burgers can be made up
  to 12 hours ahead and
  kept in the fridge.*

* *Freeze well raw.*

Measure all the burger ingredients except the chopped mint
into a bowl. Add 3 tablespoons of the chopped mint to
the bowl and season with salt and black pepper. Mix until
combined using your hands. Shape into 6 burgers.

Roll the edges of the burgers in the remaining chopped
mint to coat the outside edge. Heat the oil in a large frying
pan over a high heat. Add the burgers and fry for about
4 minutes on each side, until cooked through.

Meanwhile, mix the mint sauce and mayonnaise together
in a small bowl.

Place each burger in a brioche bun and top with some mint
mayonnaise, a few slices of dill cucumber, a slice of feta,
some rocket leaves and some mint sauce on the side.

Thyme Bavette Steak with Potatoes and Wilted Spinach

Serves 4

Bavette is the French word for flank steak. You could use whichever cut of steak you prefer, but this flat steak is full of flavour and is often called the 'butcher's cut', as they love to keep it for themselves.

4 × 170g (6oz) bavette steaks

750g (1¾lb) baby new potatoes, each sliced into £2 coin slices

3 red onions, halved and each half sliced into 8 wedges

3 tbsp olive oil

2 garlic cloves, crushed

2 tbsp chopped fresh thyme

500g (1lb 2oz) mixed coloured baby tomatoes, halved

2 tbsp balsamic glaze

A knob of butter

100g (4oz) baby spinach

Marinade

4 tbsp olive oil

2 garlic cloves, crushed

1 tbsp balsamic glaze

2 tbsp chopped fresh thyme

Mary's tips

* *Best made and served. The steak can be marinated up to 8 hours ahead.*

* *Not for freezing.*

* *Balsamic glaze is slightly thicker than balsamic vinegar so clings to the tomatoes.*

Place the steaks on a board and trim any excess membrane. If the steaks are not even in thickness, cover with cling film or baking paper and bash with a rolling pin until they are.

Measure the marinade ingredients into a bowl and mix well. Season with salt and black pepper, add the steaks and turn in the marinade to coat. Leave to marinate for about 1 hour.

Preheat the oven to 220°C/200°C fan/Gas 7. Place the potatoes, onions and 2 tablespoons of the olive oil in a single layer in a large roasting tin. Season and toss together. Roast in the oven for about 25 minutes, or until the potatoes are lightly golden.

Mix the crushed garlic and thyme together in a small bowl and sprinkle over the potatoes and onions. Push them to one end of the tin and place the tomatoes cut side up on the other. Drizzle the tomatoes with the remaining oil and the balsamic glaze. Return to the oven for 8 minutes, or until the tomatoes are just soft.

Meanwhile, heat a large frying or griddle pan until very hot. Add the steaks and fry for 1–2 minutes on each side. Spoon the excess marinade over each steak before turning. Transfer to a warm plate to rest for a few minutes. Scrape any black pieces from the pan and discard. While the steak is resting, add the butter to the pan and toss in the spinach leaves. Cook over a high heat for a few minutes until wilted.

Season the spinach and spoon into the centre of a long platter. Slice the steak into long strips and arrange on one side. Spoon the potatoes and tomatoes on the other and serve.

Glorious Beef

Serves 6

Shin of beef needs slow cooking, as it is a lean cut from the hind leg. The pickled walnuts add greatly to the flavour, but if you don't fancy them, leave them out. Use the outside sticks of celery and keep the tender centre sticks to serve with cheese.

2 tbsp sunflower oil

1kg (2¼lb) shin of beef, cut into 4cm (1½in) cubes

2 onions, roughly sliced

3 celery sticks, sliced

2 garlic cloves, crushed

50g (2oz) plain flour

450ml (¾ pint) red wine

300ml (½ pint) beef stock

1 tbsp sun-dried tomato paste

3 sprigs of thyme

1 generous tbsp redcurrant jelly

1 × 390g jar pickled walnuts, drained and quartered

200g (7oz) small chestnut mushrooms, halved

....

Mary's tips

* *Can be made a day ahead.*
* *Freezes well without the walnuts.*

Preheat the oven to 150°C/130°C fan/Gas 2.

Heat the oil in a deep ovenproof frying pan or flameproof casserole over a high heat. Add the beef and brown in two batches until sealed. Remove the beef with a slotted spoon and set aside.

Add the onions and celery to the dish and fry for 4–5 minutes. Add the garlic and fry for 30 seconds. Return the beef and any juices to the dish, season with salt and black pepper and stir.

Measure the flour into a mixing bowl. Whisk in the wine, slowly at first, until you have a smooth consistency. Add the stock, wine mixture, tomato paste and thyme sprigs to the dish. Stir and bring up to the boil. Cover with a lid and transfer to the oven for about 2½ hours, or until the meat is almost tender.

Add the redcurrant jelly, pickled walnuts and mushrooms, and return the dish to the oven for another 30 minutes.

Remove the sprigs of thyme and check the seasoning before serving with mashed potato and a green veg.

Roasted Fillet Beef
with Fresh Horseradish Sauce

Serves 6–8

A tender cut of beef is a little bit of luxury and this is the perfect main course to cook for a gathering of friends. Fillet is thought to be tricky to roast, but really it is one of the simplest. If you decide to brown the meat ahead of time and roast to serve, add 5 minutes to the cooking time.

1kg (2¼lb) middle cut thick fillet of beef

2 tbsp olive oil, plus extra to drizzle

2 tbsp Dijon mustard

4 long sprigs of rosemary

Fresh Horseradish Sauce

150ml (¼ pint) mayonnaise

150ml (¼ pint) full-fat crème fraîche

2 tsp Dijon mustard

2 tbsp peeled and grated fresh horseradish, or 3 tbsp creamed hot horseradish

....

Mary's tips

* *Beef can be fried up to 8 hours ahead and roasted to serve. If serving cold, the fillet can be roasted, carved, reassembled into it's original shape a day ahead and wrapped in cling film. This prevents the pink slices from turning grey. Ideally carve just before serving.*

* *Not for freezing.*

* *It is important to ask for a middle cut piece of fillet so the beef is an even thickness and cooks evenly.*

Preheat the oven to 220°C/200°C fan/Gas 7.

Season the fillet with plenty of salt and black pepper and rub with the oil.

Place a large frying pan over a high heat until very hot. Fry the fillet on all sides until browned.

Sit the fillet in the centre of a roasting tin and spread the mustard evenly over the top. Lay the rosemary sprigs around the fillet in the tin and drizzle the beef with oil. Roast in the oven for 20–25 minutes for medium rare (or only 15 minutes, if it is a long, thin fillet).

Remove the beef from the oven and set aside on a board. Cover with foil and leave to rest for 15 minutes. (If serving cold, leave to cool completely, then wrap in more foil and place in the fridge.)

Meanwhile, to make the sauce, measure the mayonnaise, crème fraîche and mustard into a bowl. Stir to combine, then add the horseradish. Season and mix to combine. Chill until ready to serve alongside the beef.

Carve the beef into thick or thin slices and serve with the sauce alongside.

Swiss Herb Beef and Potato Gratin

Serves 6–8

A ragu mince with a layered potato topping – this is the perfect family supper dish for all ages.
Best to use small courgettes as large ones release too much water and make the dish too sloppy.

Ragu Mince

3 tbsp sunflower oil

2 onions, chopped

1kg (2¼lb) minced beef

2 fat garlic cloves, crushed

2 tbsp tomato purée

2 × 400g tins chopped
    tomatoes

1 tsp caster sugar (optional)

Cheese Topping

1kg (2¼lb) small
    courgettes, sliced into
    1cm (½in) rounds

3 large potatoes, cut
    into 2cm (¾in) dice

300g full-fat cream cheese

1 tbsp chopped parsley

1 garlic clove, crushed

1 tbsp snipped chives

1 tbsp cornflour

1 generous tbsp
    double cream

150g (5oz) Parmesan, grated

....

Mary's tips

* *Can be made and assembled
  up to 8 hours ahead.*

* *Mince freezes well without
  the courgettes and cheese.*

Preheat the oven to 160°C/140°C fan/Gas 3. You will need
a deep 1.8 litre (3¼ pint) ovenproof dish.

Heat 2 tablespoons of the oil in a large ovenproof frying pan
or flameproof casserole over a high heat. Add the onions and
fry for a few minutes. Add the mince and brown all over.
Add the garlic and fry for 30 seconds. Stir in the tomato
purée and chopped tomatoes and season with salt and black
pepper. Cover with a lid, bring up to the boil and transfer to
the oven for 45–60 minutes, until the mince is tender. Check
the seasoning and add a little sugar if the tomatoes are sharp.
Spoon into a large ovenproof dish and level the surface.
Increase the oven temperature to 220°C/200°C fan/Gas 7.

Heat the remaining oil in a large frying pan over a medium
heat. Add the courgettes and fry in batches until golden on
both sides but not too soft. Remove from the pan with a
slotted spoon and drain on kitchen paper.

Meanwhile, boil the potatoes in boiling salted water for
3–5 minutes, until they are just cooked. Drain.

Place the cream cheese, parsley, garlic and chives in a food
processor and blend to mix together and break up the cream
cheese. Combine the cornflour and cream in a small bowl, then
add to the processor and whiz for a few seconds to mix. Season.
Spoon the cheese mixture into a bowl and add the warm
potatoes. Gently fold them together. The warm potatoes will
loosen the cheese mixture.

Arrange the courgettes in a layer over the top of the mince,
then spoon the potato mixture on top. Sprinkle with the
Parmesan and bake in the oven for about 35 minutes, or until
bubbling and golden on top.

Red Wine Beef Stew
with Horseradish Dumplings

Serves 6

So full of depth and flavour – it's worth the extra effort of making the dumplings; they make this an impressive meal in itself, needing only a green veg to serve with it.

2 tbsp olive oil

1kg (2¼lb) braising beef, cut into 5cm (2in) cubes

2 onions, chopped

3 celery sticks, sliced

2 carrots, chopped

3 garlic cloves, crushed

50g (2oz) plain flour

300ml (½ pint) red wine

300ml (½ pint) beef stock

1 tbsp chopped fresh thyme

3 bay leaves

1 tbsp redcurrant jelly

1 tbsp Worcestershire sauce

A few drops of gravy browning (optional)

1 tbsp chopped flat-leaf parsley

Horseradish Dumplings

100g (4oz) self-raising flour

50g (2oz) suet

1 tbsp chopped parsley

2 tbsp creamed hot horseradish sauce

4 tbsp water

Mary's tips

* *Stew can be made up to a day ahead. Add the dumplings to serve.*

* *Stew freezes well cooked.*

Preheat the oven to 160°C/140°C fan/Gas 3.

Heat the oil in a large ovenproof frying pan or flameproof casserole over a high heat. Add the beef and brown in two batches until sealed. Remove the beef from the dish with a slotted spoon and set aside.

Add the onions, celery and carrots to the dish and fry for a few minutes. Add the garlic and fry for 30 seconds.

Sprinkle in the flour and stir until the vegetables are coated. Gradually pour and stir in the red wine and stock. Return the beef and any juices to the dish, cover with a lid and bring up to the boil. Add the thyme, bay leaves, jelly, Worcestershire sauce and gravy browning, if using. Stir and season well with salt and black pepper. Transfer to the oven for 1½ hours, or until just tender.

Meanwhile, make the dumplings. Measure the flour, suet and a pinch of salt into a bowl, and stir together. Add the parsley, horseradish and water and mix to make a soft dough. Divide into 18 pieces and roll into little balls.

Remove the dish from the oven and sit the dumplings on top of the stew. Cover with the lid, bring back to the boil on the hob, then return to the oven for another 20 minutes, until the dumplings have risen and are cooked through. If liked, remove the lid and place the dish under a hot grill for a few minutes to brown the tops.

Sprinkle with the chopped parsley and serve piping hot with a green vegetable.

Slow Roast Whole Shoulder Lamb with Sweet Potato and Thyme

Serves 6–8

Shoulder of lamb is my favourite roast for when the family are around. I can leave it in the oven and forget about it whilst chatting and catching up on their news, which is always a joy to me.

2kg (4lb 6oz) shoulder of lamb

2 garlic cloves, cut into thin slivers

2 tbsp olive oil, plus extra to drizzle

Large bunch of thyme, leaves chopped

2 medium onions, halved and each half cut into 3 wedges

2 carrots, thickly sliced

2 celery sticks, sliced

1 litre (1¾ pints) hot lamb stock

2 large sweet potatoes, peeled and cut into 2cm (¾in) cubes

30g (1¼oz) butter

30g (1¼oz) plain flour

A few drops of gravy browning (optional)

Mary's tips

* *No need to cook ahead.*

* *Not for freezing.*

* *Roasting the veg gives flavour to the gravy.*

* *Resting the meat is so important. Giving it 20 minutes, while the squash is cooking, is the perfect amount of time for a large shoulder of lamb.*

Preheat the oven to 220°C/200°C fan/Gas 7.

Sit the lamb on a board, skin side up. Make several small holes in the meat with a knife and insert the garlic slivers into the holes. Rub the oil over the lamb, scatter over the thyme, reserving 1 tablespoon, and season well.

Place the onions, carrots and celery into the centre of a large roasting tin. Place the lamb on top, letting the vegetables act like a trivet. Roast for 30–35 minutes until brown on top.

Reduce the oven temperature to 180°C/160°C fan/Gas 4. Pour the hot stock into the tin (not over the lamb), cover the tin with foil and return to the oven for 3½–4 hours, or until completely tender and the meat is falling off the bone (see photo).

Transfer the lamb to a warm serving plate, cover tightly and leave to rest. Strain the stock and vegetables from the tin through a sieve into a jug. Discard the vegetables. Add more water or lamb stock to the jug to make up to 450ml (¾ pint).

While the lamb is resting, increase the oven temperature to 220°C/200°C fan/Gas 7. Place the potato cubes on a baking sheet, season and drizzle with oil. Roast in the oven for 20 minutes, or until golden. Sprinkle with the reserved thyme.

Meanwhile, melt the butter in a small saucepan over a medium heat. Add the flour and stir for a few seconds. Pour in the reserved stock, whisking until boiling and the gravy has thickened. Add the gravy browning, if using, and any juices from the resting lamb.Carve the lamb and serve on warm plates with the gravy and sweet potato alongside.

Cushion Lamb Stuffed with Mushroom and Mint

Serves 6

A rolled and tied shoulder of lamb is called a cushion and is a bit different to do. Ask your butcher to bone the lamb for you. The flavoursome stuffing and red wine gravy finish the dish perfectly.

About 2kg (4lb 6oz) shoulder of lamb, boned

Stuffing

A knob of butter

1 large onion, chopped

350g (12oz) chestnut mushrooms, finely chopped

2 garlic cloves, crushed

3 tbsp chopped fresh mint

100g (4oz) fresh breadcrumbs

1 egg, beaten

Gravy

1 tbsp sunflower oil, if needed

1 tbsp plain flour

100ml (3½fl oz) red wine

100ml (3½fl oz) stock

Dash of Worcestershire sauce

1 tbsp redcurrant jelly

1 tbsp tomato purée

Mary's tips

* *Can be stuffed up to a day ahead.*

* *Freezes well raw and stuffed.*

Preheat the oven to 180°C/160°C fan/Gas 4. You will need some butcher's elasticated string or normal string.

Open out the shoulder and season with salt and black pepper.

To make the stuffing, place the butter in a frying pan over a high heat. Add the onion and fry for a few minutes, then stir in the mushrooms and garlic and fry, stirring, for 3–4 minutes. Tip the mixture into a bowl and add the chopped mint, breadcrumbs and beaten egg. Season and mix until combined. Allow to cool.

Spoon the stuffing into the centre of the lamb and fold the sides over to make a cushion. Use butcher's string to tie a large ring around the middle, then tie another ring across it, like a parcel. Repeat once more. Turn over so the smooth side is up and place in a roasting tin. Roast in the oven for about 1 hour 40 minutes (20 minutes per 500g/1lb 2oz plus 20 minutes extra). Remove the lamb from the tin, cover with foil and set aside to rest.

Meanwhile, to make the gravy, place the tin over a medium heat and sprinkle in the flour (there should be fat from the lamb in the tin). Whisk over the heat for a few minutes, then gradually add the wine, whisking all the time, and bring to the boil. Add the stock, Worcestershire sauce, redcurrant jelly and tomato purée, and whisk again. Continue to boil until starting to thicken to coating consistency.

Carve the lamb and serve with the hot gravy.

Slow-cooked Lamb Stew with Herbs and Squash

Serves 6

A tender, warming casserole full of flavour and succulent meat.
The squash and sage give depth and earthy tones.

2 tbsp olive oil

1kg (2¼lb) neck fillet or shoulder of lamb, cut into 2cm (¾in) cubes

2 large onions, chopped

2 carrots, diced

2 large garlic cloves, crushed

25g (1oz) plain flour

250ml (9fl oz) white wine

300ml (½ pint) beef stock

1 tbsp redcurrant jelly

3 bay leaves

1 tbsp chopped sage

350g (12oz) butternut squash, peeled and cut into 2cm (¾in) cubes

4 tbsp chopped parsley

....

Mary's tips

* *Can be made up to a day ahead and reheated.*

* *Freezes well without the squash.*

Preheat the oven to 160°C/140°C fan/Gas 3.

Heat the oil in a large ovenproof frying pan or flameproof casserole over a high heat. Add the lamb and brown in two batches until sealed. Remove the lamb with a slotted spoon and set aside.

Add the onions and carrots to the dish and fry for 2–3 minutes. Add the garlic and fry for 30 seconds.

Measure the flour into a small bowl. Whisk in the wine to make a smooth paste. Add the wine mixture, stock and jelly to the dish and stir until boiling and thickened. Add the bay leaves and sage and return the lamb to the dish and season well with salt and black pepper. Cover with a lid and transfer to the oven for about 2 hours, or until the lamb is nearly tender.

Add the squash to the dish and continue cooking in the oven for another 30 minutes, or until the squash is cooked.

Remove the bay leaves before serving, sprinkled with chopped parsley and with mash and a green vegetable alongside.

Lamb Rogan Curry

Serves 6

This is a gentle, full-flavoured curry with Persian origins. It is worth grinding your own cardamom for an authentic flavour and mixing your own spices. If time is short, use a good-quality, shop-bought medium curry powder – about 1–2 tablespoons.

Curry Paste

10 green cardamom pods

¼ tsp ground cloves

1 tbsp ground coriander

1 tbsp ground cumin

1 tbsp paprika

2 tsp ground turmeric

1 tbsp garam marsala

4 tbsp tomato purée

1 tbsp sunflower oil

Curry

1 tbsp sunflower oil

1kg (2¼lb) boneless
   leg of lamb, cut into
   2cm (¾in) cubes

2 large onions, sliced

3 garlic cloves, crushed

1 red chilli, deseeded
   and diced

450ml (¾ pint) lamb
   or beef stock

2 cinnamon sticks

3 bay leaves

1 tbsp light muscovado sugar

150g (5oz) full-fat
   Greek yoghurt

Small bunch of
   coriander, chopped

Mary's tips

* *Can be made up to
   2 days ahead.*

* *Freezes well without
   the yoghurt.*

Preheat the oven to 150°C/130°C fan/Gas 2.

First make the curry paste. Place the cardamom pods in a small bag. Bash the pods with a rolling pin to release the seeds. Place the seeds in a pestle and mortar and grind to make a fine powder. Tip into a bowl, add the remaining paste ingredients and mix to a paste.

Heat the oil in a large ovenproof frying pan or flameproof casserole over a high heat. Add the lamb cubes and brown in two batches to seal. Remove the lamb with a slotted spoon and set aside.

Add the onions to the dish and fry for a few minutes. Add the garlic and chilli and fry for a few seconds. Return the lamb to the dish, add the curry paste and fry for a few minutes – this brings out the flavours. Pour in the stock, and add the cinnamon, bay leaves and sugar. Season with salt and black pepper, cover with a lid, bring up to the boil and transfer to the oven for about 1½ hours, or until tender.

Just before serving, add the yoghurt and stir until smooth. Remove the cinnamon and bay leaves, check the seasoning and sprinkle with the coriander. Serve with rice.

VEGGIE
MAINS

Pesto Pasta with Avocado and Broccoli

Serves 6

I am becoming more and more keen on non-meat suppers when I am at home, and the creaminess of the avocado combined with the lemony basil pesto work so well together. Serve this in small portions as it is rich but very moreish! After a long day's work, I can make this in moments and sit and eat it with my husband. Buy luxury pasta wherever possible as it has a better flavour and is more delicate than the supermarket own brands.

200g (7oz) broccoli
250g (9oz) dried tagliatelle
2 tbsp olive oil
1 onion, finely chopped
1 garlic clove, crushed
1 × 145g tub fresh pesto
1 avocado, peeled and diced
Small bunch of
  basil, chopped
Juice of ½ lemon

....

Mary's tips

* *Best made and served.*
* *Not for freezing.*

Prepare the broccoli by removing the florets and breaking them into smaller pieces. Peel the tough outer skin from the stalk and discard this, then dice the remaining stalk into cubes.

Cook the pasta in boiling salted water according to the packet instructions, adding the broccoli for the last 2 minutes of the cooking time. Drain and reserve 75ml (2½fl oz) cooking water.

Meanwhile, pour the oil into a large frying pan over a medium heat. Add the onion and garlic and fry for about 5 minutes, until soft. Stir in the pesto, pasta and broccoli, the avocado, basil, lemon juice and salt and black pepper. Gently toss together, adding enough of the reserved pasta water to make a loose sauce consistency.

Serve at once.

Roasted Veggie Filo Tart

Serves 6

The filo pastry acts as a wonderful container for the brightly flavoursome vegetables and herbs. Filo comes in different-sized sheets so make sure you layer them carefully – they need to overlap to make a firm base and sides.

2 Romano peppers, deseeded and cut into chunks

1 onion, sliced

500g (1lb 2oz) peeled butternut squash, cut into 1.5cm (⅝in) chunks

350g (12oz) cauliflower, broken into small florets

2 tbsp olive oil

150g (5oz) cherry tomatoes, halved

2 tbsp chopped fresh thyme

2 tbsp chopped fresh basil

1 tbsp balsamic vinegar

150g (5oz) Gruyère cheese, grated

3 sheets of filo (25 × 45cm/10 × 18in)

25g (1oz) butter, melted

....

Mary's tips

* *Can be made up to 4 hours ahead.*

* *Not for freezing.*

Preheat the oven to 220°C/200°C fan/Gas 7 and place a baking sheet in the oven to get hot. You will need a 23cm (9in) loose-bottomed deep cake tin.

Place the peppers, onion, squash and cauliflower in a large roasting tin. Add the oil, season well with salt and black pepper and toss to coat. Roast in the oven for 25–30 minutes, until the squash is tender.

Tip the roasted vegetables into a bowl and add the tomatoes, herbs, balsamic vinegar and 50g (2oz) of the Gruyère cheese. Toss everything together.

Lay the filo sheets on a board and brush with some of the melted butter. Place the sheets overlapping across the base and sides of the tin. Scrunch the overhanging pastry at the top edges to raise them up slightly higher than the cake tin.

Spoon the vegetables into the pastry case, sprinkle with the remaining cheese and brush the pastry edges with the remaining butter. Place the tin on the hot baking sheet in the oven and bake for 30–35 minutes, or until the pastry is golden and crisp and the top is lightly golden.

Leave to stand for 5 minutes before slicing into wedges to serve.

Roasted Squash
with Aromatic Lentils

Serves 4

A pretty veggie dish, and the little bit of spice gives the lentils a nice lift. Butternut squash have a long and narrow end by the stem and a round end where the seeds live. The round end is a bit tricky to slice evenly, as you get different shapes once the seeds have been removed, so use it to make soup on another day. It's worth reading the recipe all the way through before you start, as I've gone big on presentation!

1 small butternut squash (about 500g/1lb 2oz)

1 tbsp olive oil, plus extra for drizzling

1 banana shallot, finely chopped

1 garlic clove, crushed

1 tsp ground cumin

1 × 400g tin green lentils, drained and rinsed

2 tbsp mango chutney

1 tsp soy sauce

1 tsp balsamic vinegar

50g (2oz) fresh white breadcrumbs

25g (1oz) Parmesan, grated

Finely grated zest of ½ lemon

2 tbsp chopped parsley

....

Mary's tips

* *Can be assembled ready to go in the oven for the final cooking up to 4 hours ahead.*

* *Not for freezing.*

Preheat the oven to 200°C/180°C fan/Gas 6 and line a baking sheet with non-stick baking paper.

Cut off the long narrow end of the squash. Peel and halve the piece lengthways. Slice each one into thin slices. You will need about 400g (14oz) in total. Brush each slice with oil and arrange a quarter (100g/4oz) of the slices in an overlapping spiral shape on the baking sheet – the pieces should look like the petals of a flower. Repeat to make four flower shapes. Bake the squash in the oven for about 10 minutes, or until tender.

Meanwhile, heat the 1 tablespoon of olive oil in a frying pan over a high heat. Add the shallot and fry for a few minutes. Add the garlic and cumin and fry for a few seconds. Tip in the drained lentils and stir in the mango chutney, soy and vinegar. Continue to stir until hot through and season well with black pepper.

Remove the squash from the oven and spoon the lentil mixture into the centre of each flower, piling the mixture high, so you can see the squash petals around the edge.

Mix the breadcrumbs, Parmesan, lemon zest and parsley in a bowl then sprinkle the breadcrumb mixture on top of the lentils. Return them to the oven for another 20 minutes, or until golden around the edges and on top.

Serve piping hot with a dressed salad.

Milano Roasted Vegetable Rigatoni

Serves 4

Bursting with fresh flavours, this pasta recipe is an easy one to teach your teenagers and a great vegetarian dish, too. Alternatively, you could add crispy pancetta for the non-veggies.

4 tbsp olive oil

1 large red onion, sliced

1 yellow pepper, halved and deseeded

1 red pepper, halved and deseeded

600g (1lb 5oz) cherry tomatoes, halved

4 garlic cloves, finely sliced

1 red chilli, deseeded and roughly chopped

6 sprigs of thyme, leaves chopped

2 tbsp sun-dried tomato paste

Small bunch of basil, leaves chopped

1 tbsp balsamic vinegar

250g (9oz) rigatoni

1 ball of buffalo mozzarella, torn into pieces

....

Mary's tips

* *Best made and served.*

* *Not for freezing.*

Preheat the oven to 200°C/180°C fan/Gas 6.

Measure 2 tablespoons of the oil into a medium roasting tin and add the onion, peppers, tomatoes, garlic, chilli and thyme and season well with salt and black pepper. Turn the veg to coat in the oil, then roast in the oven for about 30 minutes, or until the onion has gone soft.

Leave the veg to cool slightly, then remove the skins from the peppers and tomatoes and discard. Roughly chop the peppers into small dice and add back to the roasting tin with the tomatoes. Squish the tomatoes with a fork, add the sun-dried tomato paste, basil and balsamic vinegar and mix well.

Cook the pasta in boiling salted water according to the packet instructions. Drain and return to the pan. Tip the pepper mixture into the pan with the pasta, add the mozzarella and toss to combine.

Pile into a bowl and serve hot.

For the Love of...Vegetables

Carrots

Baby carrots are my favourite, sweet
and delicious raw or cooked. They are
so versatile, too. With their wonderful,
green, feathered tops, they are a joy
to grow at home.

Celeriac

Celeriac and celery are from the same
family and have a similar flavour but
are very different in shape and cooking
properties. Celeriac is a knobbly round
vegetable with a nutty flavour. Grown as
a root bulb with green leaves, the flesh is
firm and is good for soups, purées, boiling,
roasting and is the hero of the classic
French dish remoulade. Celery is a natural
with cheese and makes a lovely, fresh
alternative to oatcakes and crackers.

Cauliflower

Very reasonable to buy, cauliflower is
right back in fashion. Cauliflower cheese
is a classic and a few small florets are a
great addition to any vegetable soup.
My latest favourite way to cook cauliflower
is to cut thick slices from the centre
and roast or pan fry them. Cauliflower
lends itself to be tossed in a little ground
coriander and cumin before frying, as it
can handle strong flavours.

New Potatoes

My favourite potatoes are the first Jersey
Royals, which are the finest baby potatoes
and come in season in late spring and are
worth the wait. The Cornish variation
follows in early summer and is also
wonderful. Simply boiled and served with
butter and chopped mint – delicious!

Mushrooms

We are so lucky to have such a wide variety of mushrooms available to us. I love to forage with the family in September, when mushrooms are growing freely in the fields – a puffball is the ultimate foraging reward! Never eat wild mushrooms without having first had them identified by someone who knows, though. The classic button, chestnut and close cup are favourites for holding their shape when cooked. Oyster and shiitake mushrooms are more delicate in flavour and texture, so are better for quick cooking in stir fries, along with Wild Alexanders and beech mushrooms, too. Portobello mushrooms used whole are fabulous stuffed. Mushrooms can release water when cooking, though, so be sure to drive off any excess liquid to keep the best flavour.

Onions And Leeks

I prefer white onions for cooking. Check the outer layer is not too tough – if grown from seed rather than sets, they tend to have a tough outer layer. Red onions are nice raw in a salad or used in a marinade, but tend to turn grey and lose their lovely pink colour when cooked. Onion skins are good to add when making stock, as they give a lovely golden colour. Leeks are best bought medium or small, as the larger ones can be tough and need longer to cook. Wash them well before cooking, though, as soil can settle between the layers.

Squashes

Squash come in many shapes, sizes and colours, and look fabulous in an autumn fruit bowl. My favourite is butternut, which is bright orange in colour and has a firm texture. It is good for boiling and roasting as it holds its shape. Acorn squash have yellow-orange flesh, while gem are tiny with white flesh and originate from South Africa. For a quick vegetable side dish, cut a squash or pumpkin in half, scoop out the seeds, drizzle with oil, season and roast. Scoop out the flesh to use in soups and purées, or serve in slices.

Shallots

I am keen on banana shallots, which are the long rather than round ones. They are easier to peel and are slightly less sharp in flavour than the tiny round ones.

Double Mushroom Stroganoff

Serves 4

A classic stroganoff is made with beef, but I love this version with mushrooms.
It makes a lovely lunch dish with a little rice and a side of salad leaves.

A knob of butter

800g (1¾lb) mixed button
and small chestnut
mushrooms, halved

2 garlic cloves, crushed

1 tbsp paprika

300ml (½ pint) pouring
double cream

1 tbsp Dijon mustard

1 tsp Worcestershire sauce

Juice of ½ lemon

3 tbsp chopped parsley

1 tsp caster sugar, or to taste

Small handful of
gherkins, chopped, to
garnish (optional)

....

Mary's tips

* *Best made and served.*

* *Not for freezing.*

Place a large frying pan over a high heat until hot. Add
the butter and, when it is foaming, stir in the mushrooms.
Cover with a lid and cook for 2–3 minutes. Remove the lid,
stir and continue to fry over a high heat for about 1 minute,
to drive off the liquid and brown the mushrooms.

Add the garlic and paprika and fry for 30 seconds. Stir in
the cream, mustard, Worcestershire sauce and season with
salt and black pepper. Bring to the boil, then reduce the heat
and simmer for a few minutes, until the sauce has a coating
consistency.

Stir in the lemon juice, chopped parsley and sugar to taste.

Sprinkle with chopped gherkins, if using, and serve with rice.

Roasted Vegetable and Coconut Curry

Serves 6

I love a veggie curry and this dish with root vegetables and a creamy coconut sauce is one of my favourites. If I'm having friends round, I serve this with a selection of other curries, such as Lamb Rogan on page 133 and Kashmiri Chicken on page 74.

500g (1lb 2oz) peeled celeriac, cut into 2cm (¾in) cubes

250g (9oz) parsnips, peeled and cut into 2cm (¾in) cubes

3 tbsp sunflower oil

2 onions, sliced

A large knob of fresh root ginger, peeled and finely grated

1 red chilli, deseeded and finely diced

2 tbsp medium curry powder

1 tsp ground turmeric

2 × 400g tins full-fat coconut milk

1 tbsp mango chutney

200g (7oz) French beans, each sliced into 3

Small bunch of coriander, chopped

....

Mary's tips

* *Can be made up to a day ahead but add the green beans just before serving so they keep their bright green colour.*

* *Not for freezing.*

Preheat the oven to 220°C/200°C fan/Gas 7.

Place the celeriac and parsnip cubes in a large roasting tin. Drizzle 2 tablespoons of the oil over the top and season well with salt and black pepper. Roast in the oven for 20–25 minutes, until just tender.

Heat the remaining oil in a large ovenproof frying pan or flameproof casserole over a high heat. Add the onions and fry for 5 minutes. Add the ginger, chilli, curry powder and turmeric and fry for a few seconds, then pour in the coconut milk. Add the mango chutney and season well. Bring up to the boil, then reduce the heat, cover and simmer for about 10 minutes, or until the onions are almost tender. Add the roasted vegetables and simmer for a further 5 minutes.

Meanwhile, cook the beans in boiling salted water for 3 minutes. Drain and add to the curry with the coriander.

Check the seasoning and serve with basmati rice.

Aubergine Caponata

Serves 4

Traditionally made with green olives and red wine vinegar, I prefer using soft black pitted olives and white wine vinegar, as I always have them in the cupboard.

8 tbsp olive oil

2 aubergines, cut into 2cm (¾in) cubes

2 onions, finely chopped

2 celery sticks, finely chopped

1 red pepper, deseeded and cut into 1cm (½in) cubes

3 large garlic cloves, crushed

500g (1lb 2oz) passata

100g (4oz) soft pitted black olives

2 tbsp white wine vinegar

3 tbsp capers

1½ tbsp caster sugar

3 tbsp chopped parsley

....

Mary's tips

* *Can be made up to a day ahead and reheated to serve.*

* *Freezes for up to a month.*

Heat 3 tablespoons of the oil in a large frying pan over a high heat. Add half of the aubergine cubes and fry until browned. Remove the aubergine from the pan and set aside. Heat another 3 tablespoons of the oil and fry the remaining aubergine. Set aside with the rest.

Heat the remaining oil in the pan. Add the onions, celery and pepper and fry over a high heat for 3–4 minutes. Add the garlic and fry for a few seconds. Return the aubergine to the pan, add the passata, olives, vinegar, capers and sugar. Season with salt and black pepper, cover with a lid and bring up to the boil. Reduce the heat and simmer gently for 20–25 minutes. Remove the lid and simmer for another 5 minutes, until the sauce has reduced and the vegetables are soft but not mushy.

Sprinkle with parsley and serve with crusty bread, couscous or as a vegetable side dish.

Plant Burger

Makes 8 burgers

Full of flavour and spice, this burger will be loved by meat eaters and vegetarians alike. Puy lentils are one of my favourite pulses, but they do need a bit of flavour adding to pep them up! Be careful when turning the burgers, as they have a delicate texture and could crumble.

200g (7oz) cauliflower, broken into small florets

4 tbsp sunflower oil

1 large onion, finely chopped

200g (7oz) chestnut mushrooms, diced

1 × 250g packet cooked puy lentils

2 garlic cloves, crushed

½ red chilli, deseeded and diced

100g (4oz) sun-dried tomatoes, chopped

1 tsp ground cumin

Plain flour, for coating

8 brioche buns, split in half

Topping

Handful of watercress

2 beefsteak tomatoes, sliced

2 tbsp hummus

....

Mary's tips

* *Can be made ahead up to a day ahead.*

* *Freeze well uncooked.*

Blanch the cauliflower in boiling salted water for 3 minutes, then drain and refresh under cold water. Drain again.

Heat 2 tablespoons of the oil in a frying pan over a high heat. Add the onion and fry for a few minutes. Add the mushrooms and fry until the liquid has evaporated. Add the puy lentils, garlic and chilli and fry for 3 minutes. Remove from the heat and leave to cool.

Place the tomatoes in a food processor and whiz until finely chopped. Add the cauliflower and mushroom and lentil mixture to the tomatoes and season with cumin, salt and black pepper. Pulse briefly until the mixture is finely chopped, but still with texture. Be careful not to purée the mixture.

Shape into 8 burgers, coat in flour and place in the fridge to chill for 30 minutes.

Heat the remaining oil in a large frying pan over a high heat. Add the burgers and fry for 3–4 minutes on each side, until golden brown, turning carefully halfway through.

Serve in the buns with watercress, tomato and some hummus.

Beach Hut Mushrooms and Spinach on Toast

Serves 6

This is just my sort of lunch or light supper dish, and a great idea for camping and cooking on a gas stove. I adore mushrooms and the combination of mushroom flavour and crunchy sourdough gives so much joy to the dish. Banana shallots are larger than regular shallots and I prefer them, as they are easier to peel and slightly milder in flavour. The mushroom mixture is delicious on toasted rye bread, too.

2 tbsp sunflower oil

A knob of butter

1 banana shallot, thinly sliced

200g (7oz) chestnut mushrooms, sliced

200g (7oz) small button mushrooms, sliced

175g (6oz) shiitake mushrooms, sliced

1 large garlic clove, crushed

150ml (¼ pint) double cream

6 slices sourdough bread

200g (7oz) baby spinach

6 sun-blushed tomatoes, snipped into small pieces

1 tbsp chopped parsley

Mary's tips

* Best made and served.

* Not for freezing.

Heat the oil and butter in a large frying pan over a high heat. Add the shallot and fry for 3 minutes. Add all the mushrooms and the garlic and fry for 2 minutes. Cover with a lid and cook for 2 minutes. Remove the lid and continue to fry for a few minutes to drive off the liquid.

Pour in the double cream and stir gently until the cream has reduced to a thick, coating consistency. Season well with salt and black pepper.

Meanwhile, toast the bread and arrange on plates. Divide the mushrooms between the slices of toast.

Place the spinach in the unwashed pan with 1 tablespoon of water. Fry quickly over a high heat until wilted. Season and arrange a small pile on top of each mushroom toast. Sprinkle with the sun-blushed tomatoes and parsley and serve straight away.

Roasted Romano Peppers
with Puy Lentils and Feta

Serves 6

These are wonderful as a main dish for vegetarians or as a side dish for
a buffet or BBQ. Romano peppers are long, mild red peppers.

100g (4oz) dried puy lentils

2 large garlic cloves, crushed

2 tbsp balsamic vinegar

3 tbsp sun-dried
    tomato paste

1 tbsp chopped fresh oregano

4 tbsp chopped fresh parsley

4 spring onions, sliced

8 Peppadew peppers,
    chopped

100g (4oz) cherry
    tomatoes, quartered

150g (5oz) feta cheese,
    crumbled

3 large Romano peppers

2 tbsp olive oil, plus
    extra for greasing

....

Mary's tips

* *Can be assembled up
    to 6 hours ahead and
    cooked to serve.*

* *Not for freezing.*

Preheat the oven to 200°C/180°C fan/Gas 6 and grease
a roasting tin.

Cook the lentils in boiling water according to the packet
instructions. Drain and tip into a bowl.

Add the garlic, vinegar, sun-dried tomato paste, herbs,
spring onions, Peppadew peppers, tomatoes and 100g
(4oz) of the feta cheese to the lentils. Season well with
black pepper and mix well.

Slice the Romano peppers in half lengthways through the
stem, keeping them intact, and remove the seeds. Divide
the lentil filling between the pepper halves and place in the
prepared tin. Sprinkle the remaining feta cheese over the
top and drizzle with the oil. Roast in the oven for about
25 minutes, or until the feta is tinged brown and the
peppers are soft but still holding their shape.

Roasted Pepper, Beetroot and Feta Oval Tart

Serves 6

Often called a galette, this puff pastry tart is vibrant to look at and layering the flavours makes it easy to prepare. You can buy the beetroot ready-cooked, or you can boil your own. If you do, leave the roots on and cut off the leaves 10cm (4 in) above the beetroot bulb. This prevents the colour bleeding out into the cooking water and causing the beetroot to be less red in colour.

1 yellow pepper, halved and deseeded

1 red pepper, halved and deseeded

1 × 320g sheet of all-butter puff pastry

3 tbsp sun-dried tomato paste

2 garlic cloves, crushed

200g (7oz) feta cheese, finely crumbled

600g (1lb 5oz) cooked and peeled beetroot, thinly sliced into rounds

4 tbsp olive oil

1 tbsp balsamic vinegar

50g (2oz) rocket leaves

....

Mary's tips

* *Can be assembled up to 4 hours ahead.*

* *Not for freezing.*

* *Covering the bowl of peppers in cling film helps them steam and therefore the skins peel off easily. You could place them in a sealed plastic bag, if preferred.*

Preheat the oven to 220°C/200°C fan/Gas 7. You will need two baking sheets with non-stick baking paper.

Put the pepper halves cut side down on to one baking sheet. Roast for about 30 minutes, or until the skins are brown. Place in a bowl, cover with cling film and leave to cool. Peel off the skins and discard. Thinly slice the peppers into long strips.

Dust the worktop with flour, unroll the pastry sheet and roll it so it is slightly thinner. Cut out an oval shape from the sheet measuring about 36 × 24cm (14¼ × 9½in). Place on the lined baking sheet and twist the edges of the pastry to make an informal border and crimp, if you like. Prick the base with a fork.

Mix the sun-dried tomato paste with the garlic in a small bowl. Spread over the base of the pastry. Scatter the feta on top. Arrange the beetroot in a neat overlapping spiral so it covers the base. Season well with salt and black pepper, brush with 1 tablespoon of the oil and bake in the oven for 25–30 minutes, or until the pastry is crisp underneath and around the edges.

Meanwhile, mix the vinegar, the remaining olive oil and a little salt in a bowl. Add the rocket and toss to coat. Place the rocket in a pile in the middle of the tart, then scatter the peppers over the top. Serve hot.

SALADS
AND SIDES

Brown Rice with Courgette Ribbons

Serves 4

Different and healthy, the mint yoghurt dressing adds a lovely texture and is full of flavour. The courgette ribbons give wonderful colour and look so pretty.

150g (5oz) brown rice

2 celery sticks, finely sliced

1 large red onion,
  finely chopped

2 carrots, grated

Small bunch of
  coriander, chopped

150g (5oz) pomegranate
  seeds

1 large courgette, peeled
  into ribbons

Mint Yoghurt Dressing

1½ tbsp Dijon mustard

2 tbsp white wine vinegar

6 tbsp olive oil

Juice of ½ lemon

Caster sugar, to taste

Small bunch of mint,
  leaves chopped

200g (7oz) natural yoghurt

....

Mary's tips

* *Can be assembled up
  to 4 hours ahead.*

* *Not for freezing.*

Cook the rice in boiling salted water according to the packet instructions. Drain, then run under cold water. Drain again and set aside to cool.

To make the dressing, measure the mustard, vinegar, oil, lemon juice and sugar, to taste, into a bowl. Whisk and season well with salt and black pepper. Add half of the chopped mint and whisk again. Reserve 2 tablespoons of the dressing and set aside. Add the yoghurt to the remaining dressing in the bowl and mix well.

Place the cooled rice, celery, onion, carrots, coriander, pomegranate seeds and the remaining chopped mint in a bowl. Add the yoghurt dressing, season and mix well. Spoon into a serving dish.

Add the courgette ribbons to the reserved herb dressing and toss to coat. Arrange the courgettes on top of the salad to serve.

Golden Crunchy Thyme Parsnips

Serves 4–6

Crunchy sweet parsnips – the perfect side dish. The addition
of semolina gives them a lovely crispy outside.

4 large parsnips (about
   500g/1lb 2oz), peeled and
   cut into 5cm (2in) strips

3 tbsp sunflower oil

25g (1oz) semolina

1 tbsp paprika

1 tbsp chopped fresh thyme

....

Mary's tips

* *Best made and served.*
* *Not for freezing.*

Cook the parsnips in boiling water for 4 minutes. Drain and
leave to cool.

Preheat the oven to 220°C/200°C fan/Gas 7. Add 1 tablespoon
of the oil to a roasting tin and place in the oven for 5 minutes
to get hot.

Add the remaining oil to a bowl. Season the parsnips with
salt and black pepper and toss in the oil to coat.

Mix the semolina, paprika and thyme together in a small
bowl. Add to the parsnips and mix well to coat them in
the mixture.

Place the parsnips in one layer in the tin with the hot oil and
roast for about 20 minutes, turning over halfway through
the cooking time, until golden and crisp.

Lightly Spiced Pilau Rice

Serves 4

The perfect rice to serve with a curry – try this with Kashmiri Chicken on page 74 or Lamb Rogan on page 133. Pick out the cardamon pods before serving, if you prefer.

1 tbsp sunflower oil

1 large onion, finely chopped

1 tsp ground turmeric

1 tsp ground cumin

275g (10oz) basmati
   rice, rinsed

½ tsp salt

12 cardamom pods, bashed

6 spring onions, finely sliced

50g (2oz) pistachio nuts,
   slivered or finely chopped

....

Mary's tips

* *Can be made an hour
   ahead and kept warm.*

* *Not for freezing.*

Heat the oil in a shallow wide-based saucepan over a high heat. Add the onion and fry for a few minutes, then sprinkle in the turmeric and cumin and fry for 1 minute.

Add the rinsed rice to the pan and coat in the oil, onion and spices. Pour in 500ml (18fl oz) water, add the salt and cardamom pods and stir once, then cover with a lid. Bring up to the boil, then reduce the heat and simmer very gently for 10 minutes.

Turn off the heat and leave with the lid on for another 10 minutes, until all the liquid has been absorbed and the rice is fluffy and cooked.

Stir in the spring onions and scatter the pistachios over the top to serve.

Jasmine Lemongrass Rice

Serves 4

Jasmine rice is a kind of sticky rice and is perfect to serve with curries.
The lemongrass infuses the rice to give a wonderful aroma and flavour.

250g (9oz) jasmine rice
½ tsp salt
2 lemongrass stalks, bashed

....

Mary's tips

* *Best made and served.*
* *Not for freezing.*

Place the rice in a sieve and run under cold water to remove some of the starch.

Tip into a saucepan, add the salt and lemongrass and pour in 450ml (¾ pint) water. Cover with a lid and bring up to the boil. Stir once, then reduce the heat and simmer for 12–15 minutes, until the rice is fluffy and nearly all the water is absorbed.

Turn off the heat and leave to stand for 10 minutes, or until all the water has been absorbed.

Remove the lemongrass and fluff the rice with a fork to serve.

Potato and Parsnip Gratin

Serves 6

Delicious and luxurious, this potato and parsnip dish will become your new favourite.
It is similar to Dauphinoise but the veg are cut into long, chunky pieces, rather than
thin slices. Use pouring double cream as it blends with the vegetables more easily.

750g (1¾lb) medium-
sized potatoes, peeled

500g (1lb 2oz)
parsnips, peeled

25g (1oz) butter, plus
extra for greasing

1 fat garlic clove, crushed

300ml (½ pint) double cream

75g (3oz) Parmesan, grated

....

Mary's tips

* *Can be assembled up
to 8 hours ahead. Best
cooked to serve.*

* *Not for freezing.*

Preheat the oven to 200°C/180°C fan/Gas 6 and butter
a 30 × 23cm (12 × 9in) ovenproof dish.

Slice each potato into 6–8 evenly sized wedges. Slice the
parsnips into similarly sized shapes.

Blanch the potatoes in a large saucepan of boiling salted
water for 3 minutes. Add the parsnips to the potatoes in the
pan and continue to boil for a further 3 minutes. Drain well.

Return the veg to the pan and add the butter. Place over a
medium heat and, once the butter has melted, add the garlic
and cook for 1 minute. Toss the potatoes and parsnips to
coat in the butter. Season well with salt and black pepper,
then tip into the prepared dish. Bake in the oven for about
20 minutes, or until the vegetables are just starting to brown.

Pour the cream over the veg and sprinkle with the Parmesan.
Return to the oven for another 15 minutes, or until lightly
golden and crisp on top.

Serve hot.

Crispy Roasted Sweet Potatoes

Serves 4

Something a bit different to traditional roast potatoes. The added semolina gives
the potatoes a crispy, crunchy outside and helps to hold them together.

4 tbsp sunflower oil

700g (1lb 9oz) peeled
sweet potatoes, sliced
into 4cm (1½in) pieces

About 2 tbsp semolina

....

Mary's tips

* *Best made and served
straight away.*

* *Not for freezing.*

Preheat the oven to 220°C/200°C fan/Gas 7.

Pour 3 tablespoons of the oil into a large shallow roasting
tin and slide into the oven for about 5 minutes, or until
piping hot.

Meanwhile, place the sweet potatoes and the remaining
oil in a mixing bowl. Turn the pieces to coat in the oil.
Sprinkle in the semolina, season with salt and black pepper
and turn again, until they are lightly dusted.

Tip the sweet potatoes into the roasting tin in a single layer
and roast for 15 minutes. Remove from the oven, turn the
potatoes and continue to roast for a further 10–15 minutes,
until brown and crispy.

Yorkshire Pudding

Serves 8

An old faithful that always works if you have very hot oil and a very hot oven. We find it best to be generous with the eggs to give the best rise. You can use any oil you wish, but I find goose or duck fat give the best flavour and are a must with roast beef.

100g (4oz) plain flour

¼ tsp salt

3 large eggs

225ml (8fl oz) semi-skimmed milk

About 120ml (4fl oz) sunflower oil, goose or duck fat or beef dripping

....

Mary's tips

* *The puddings can be made completely ahead and reheated in a hot oven for about 8 minutes. The batter can be made up to 2 hours ahead.*

* *Freeze well cooked.*

Preheat the oven 220°C/200°C fan/Gas 7. You will need a either a 12-hole deep bun tin or 2 × 4-hole large Yorkshire pudding tins.

Measure the flour and salt into a bowl and make a well in the centre. Add the eggs and a little of the milk. Whisk until smooth, then gradually add the remaining milk, whisking all the time, until bubbles burst on the surface. This can be done by hand but is best with an electric whisk. Pour into a jug.

Measure a dessertspoon of oil or dripping into each hole of the tin. Transfer to the oven for 5–10 minutes, or until piping hot (the time will depend on the thickness of the tin).

Carefully remove from the oven and divide the batter evenly between the holes. Return to the oven and cook for 20–25 minutes, or until golden brown and well risen.

Serve immediately.

Crushed Small Garlic Potatoes

Serves 6

Another exciting way to serve one of our favourite vegetables – the potato!

750g (1¾lb) baby
   new potatoes
1 tbsp olive oil
50g (2oz) butter
2 garlic cloves, crushed

....

Mary's tips

* *Potatoes can be crushed up to 2 hours ahead ready for roasting.*

* *Not for freezing.*

Preheat the oven to 220°C/200°C fan/Gas 7.

Place the new potatoes in a saucepan. Cover with cold salted water and bring to the boil. Boil for about 15 minutes, until just cooked. Drain, then squash each potato gently with the back of a fork, until slightly crushed.

Place a roasting tin in the oven for 5 minutes to get hot.

Add the oil, butter and garlic to the tin and swirl them around, until the butter has melted. Tip in the potatoes and swirl again to coat. Roast in the oven for 25–30 minutes, until golden brown and little crispy.

Magical Prepare Ahead
Platter of Vegetables

Serves 6

This is a wonderful way to serve a selection of vegetables without having to wash loads of pots and pans afterwards. They can be prepared ahead and cooked to serve.

A knob of butter,
  for greasing

1 medium butternut
  squash, peeled and cut
  into 2cm (¾in) cubes

2 tbsp olive oil

500g (1lb 2oz) peeled
  potatoes, cut into cubes

500g (1lb 2oz) peeled
  celeriac, cut into cubes

2 tbsp crème fraîche

150g (5oz) sugar snap
  peas, destringed and
  cut in half lengthways

250g (9oz) tenderstem
  broccoli

300g (10½oz) petits pois

....

Mary's tips

* *Can be prepared up
  to 12 hours ahead.*

* *Not for freezing.*

* *It is so important for the
  green vegetables to be
  refreshed in cold water –
  this stops the cooking and
  therefore sets the bright
  green colour. Reheating
  to serve doesn't cook the
  vegetables any more, it
  just gets them piping hot.*

Preheat the oven to 200°C/180°C fan/Gas 6. Line a baking sheet with non-stick baking paper and butter an ovenproof platter.

Scatter the squash on to the baking sheet and drizzle the olive oil over the top. Season well with salt and black pepper and toss to coat. Roast in the oven for about 30 minutes, or until soft and golden brown.

Boil the potatoes in a large saucepan of boiling salted water for 5 minutes, then add the celeriac and boil for a further 10 minutes, until both are tender. Drain well and return to the pan. Season well, add the crème fraîche and purée until smooth using a stick blender, or place in a food processor and whiz until just smooth.

Blanch the sugar snaps, broccoli and peas together in boiling salted water for 2 minutes. Drain and refresh in cold water, then drain again. Remove the broccoli stems and keep them separate.

Arrange the vegetables in rows on the prepared ovenproof platter – a row of the celeriac and potato purée, a row of the broccoli stems, a row of butternut squash and a row of mixed petits pois and sugar snaps. Cover with buttered foil and place in the fridge to chill until ready to reheat.

When ready to serve, preheat the oven to 200°C/180°C fan/Gas 6 and bring the vegetables to room temperature, keeping the foil on.

Cook in the oven for about 20 minutes, or until piping hot.

Potato Salad
with Fennel and Mustard

Serves 6–8

A twist on the classic potato salad we used to have when my children were young.
The fennel gives a crunch, the mustard adds sharpness and the dill pickle sweetness.
Dill pickles come in a jar like gherkins but are sweeter and more tender.

750g (1¾lb) baby
   new potatoes

2 tbsp Dijon mustard

2 tbsp white wine vinegar

2 tsp runny honey

4 tbsp olive oil

4 spring onions, sliced

1 small fennel bulb,
   thinly sliced

2 celery sticks, thinly sliced

4 tbsp crème fraîche

4 tbsp chopped parsley

50g (2oz) dill pickles,
   finely chopped

....

Mary's tips

* *Can be made up to
6 hours ahead.*

* *Not for freezing.*

Cook the new potatoes in boiling salted water for about
15 minutes, or until just tender. Drain and cool slightly
before removing the skins, if liked. Slice the potatoes in half
or into quarters.

Measure the mustard, vinegar, honey and oil into a bowl.
Whisk together. Add the warm potatoes, spring onions,
fennel and celery, and mix well. Season with salt and black
pepper. Cover and chill in the fridge for about an hour.

When ready to serve, mix the crème fraîche, parsley and
dill pickles together in a bowl and season well. Add to the
potatoes and stir to combine.

Serve at room temperature.

Roasted Fennel, Dill and Bean Salad with Lemon Dressing

Serves 4–6

Full of colour and flavour, this salad will be a joy to hand around. I love fennel bulbs, and marinating and cooking helps to soften the flavour and tenderise them.

2 fennel bulbs

2 tbsp olive oil

2 red peppers, deseeded and sliced into large pieces

1 red onion, thinly sliced

1 × 400g tin cannellini beans, drained and rinsed

Small bunch of dill, chopped

Lemon Dressing

Juice of ½ large lemon

1 tbsp white wine vinegar

4 tbsp olive oil

Caster sugar, to taste

....

Mary's tips

* *Can be assembled up to 4 hours ahead. Dress to serve. Dressing can be made up to 4 days ahead.*

* *Not for freezing.*

Preheat the oven to 220°C/200°C fan/Gas 7.

Trim the base and stalks from the fennel bulbs. Slice them in half lengthways, then slice each half into 6 wedges through the core.

Blanch the fennel in a pan of boiling salted water for 3 minutes. Drain well.

Measure the oil into a large roasting tin and slide into the oven for 5 minutes to get hot.

Add the fennel and peppers to the tin, spreading them out in a single layer. Season well with salt and black pepper and roast for about 15 minutes, or until golden underneath. Turn the vegetables and roast for another 5–8 minutes, until browned. Leave to cool in the tin.

Meanwhile, measure the dressing ingredients into a jug. Whisk everything together, then add the red onion and season well. Leave to marinate for 10 minutes.

Arrange the fennel and peppers on a serving platter. Scatter the beans and dill on top, then pour over the dressing to serve.

For the Love of...Greens

Lettuce

I adore lettuce and my favourite varieties
are Little Gem and Romaine. They
make a good base for salads and I like to
add rocket for its peppery flavour. Break
lettuce into pieces, rather than slicing
it, and only dress it just before serving,
otherwise it will wilt. Lamb's lettuce
is best kept as the whole plant, so just
rip off the root and include in a green
salad for added interest. Micro lettuce
are seeds grown in small containers or
bowls and make a lovely addition to a
salad, sandwich or as a garnish, adding a
different texture. You can be brave and try
an unusual flavour, as you only use a small
amount – such as wasabi rocket, chilli
mesclun or pea shoots. Micro greens, like
beets, celery and herbs, are easy to grow,
too. I remember growing cress in a small
pot on the windowsill as a child and it is
fashionable again, but now there are many
different varieties. It is wonderful to do
this with children, to share with them a
love of growing their own food. They can
have fun cutting some and watching it
shoot up again.

Petit Pois,
Sugar Snap Peas and
Mange Tout

It is always uselful to have a bag of
petits pois in the freezer. Sweet and
delicate, they are a great vegetable to be
mixed with sugar snap peas and mange
tout. Sugar snap peas and larger mange
tout can need destringing and I like to
cut them in half lengthways or on the
diagonal before cooking, so the peas can
be seen inside the pods.

Pointed or
Sweetheart Cabbage

For me, these are the king of cabbages.
Shredded, boiled briefly in salted water,
then drained and tossed in butter with a
little pepper, it is hard to beat.

Purple Sprouting and Tenderstem Broccoli

Briefly cooked in lightly salted water, tenderstem and purple sprouting broccoli are both joyful. I cook the ends of the stalks for our dogs, as I'm told it's very good for them!

Samphire and Asparagus

Samphire and asparagus are both special and need to be treated with respect. Samphire, naturally growing wild by our coastlines, have delicate fronds that need trimming from the base, if they are long. Cook them in boiling water for only 2 minutes, to keep the bright colour and freshness. Add butter just before serving. The British asparagus season is May to June and it is wonderful to wait for the season to start, in order to taste the best asparagus. There are many pick your own asparagus farms, too, which is the best way to buy them.

Spinach

Baby spinach is wonderful as it can be eaten raw in a salad or wilted in a flash to serve as a vegetable. If using home-grown or older spinach, it is best to cut out the stalk, then roll the leaves into tubes and shred them finely. I grow perpetual spinach at home, which is slow to go to seed.

Asparagus, Parmesan and Pistachio Salad

Serves 4–6

A simple salad but when made with love and care it becomes a luxury. Simplicity at its best. Shavings of Parmesan are easy to make from a slab of cheese using a vegetable peeler.

250g (9oz) asparagus spears

1 × 60g packet rocket leaves

50g (2oz) Parmesan, thin shavings

50g (2oz) pistachio nuts, slivered or roughly chopped

Garlic Vinaigrette Dressing

1 tbsp Dijon mustard

2 tbsp white wine vinegar

1 tbsp balsamic glaze

6 tbsp olive or sunflower oil

1 small garlic clove, crushed

1 tsp caster sugar, to taste

....

Mary's tips

* *Assemble up to 4 hours ahead and dress just before serving.*

* *Not for freezing.*

Break the woody ends from the asparagus spears and discard. Slice off the tips and cut the stalks on the diagonal into four slices. Blanch the asparagus in boiling salted water for 2 minutes, then drain and run under cold water until cold. Drain again.

Place the rocket in a salad bowl or serving plate. Scatter the asparagus on top. Sprinkle with the cheese and pistachio nuts.

Measure all the vinaigrette ingredients into a jug and add 2 tablespoons of cold water. Lightly whisk everything together and season with salt and black pepper.

Pour the dressing over the salad just before serving.

Grilled Courgette and Artichoke Salad with Mint Dressing

Serves 4–6

A fresh-tasting salad, this is a meal in itself, or perfect as a side dish. The mint dressing gives it a lovely lift. Chargrilled artichoke hearts can be bought in the deli section of most supermarkets or from your local deli.

2 long, thin courgettes, cut on the diagonal into long, thin slices

2 tbsp olive oil

1 red pepper, halved and deseeded

1 Little Gem lettuce

1 × 280g jar sliced chargrilled artichoke hearts

Small bunch of mint, leaves finely chopped

1 tbsp capers

1 ripe avocado, peeled and sliced into long strips

Juice of ½ lemon

Dressing

2 tbsp white wine vinegar

1 tsp grainy mustard

1½ tsp runny honey

Mary's tips

* *Can be assembled up to 4 hours ahead. Add the avocado, dressing and lemon juice just before serving.*

* *Not for freezing.*

Preheat the grill to high and line a large baking sheet with tin foil.

Brush the courgette slices on both sides with olive oil. Season well with salt and black pepper and arrange in a single layer on the baking sheet. Place the pepper cut side down at one end of the baking sheet.

Grill for 5–10 minutes, or until the courgettes are golden brown. Turn the courgettes and grill for another 5 minutes, or until the courgettes are golden and the pepper is black. Place the pepper in a bowl, cover with cling film and leave to cool. Once the pepper has cooled, peel off and discard the skin, then thinly slice.

Separate the leaves from the lettuce. Thinly shred the white part and break the top off the leaves in pieces.

Place the lettuce in a serving dish and scatter the courgettes and peppers on top. Drain the artichokes from the jar (reserving the oil for the dressing) and arrange over the veg. Scatter half the mint leaves and the capers on top, then season with black pepper and sea salt flakes.

Place the artichoke oil in a bowl, add the remaining chopped mint and all the dressing ingredients and whisk. Carefully add the avocado slices and turn to coat.

Tip the dressing and avocado over the salad just before serving and finish by squeezing the lemon over the top.

Samphire and Double Bean Salad

Serves 4–6

The mustard garlic dressing gives the salad a big lift. Found in marshes by the sea, growing naturally along marsh beds and waterways, samphire is a new favourite. Thin green stalks that are salty and fresh, it goes perfectly with fish and you'll find it by the fresh fish section in good supermarkets. Removing the broad beans from their skins takes a little time but is so worth it – it's a great job to give children to do to help.

500g (1lb 2oz) frozen
   baby broad beans
180g (6oz) samphire
1 × 400g tin cannellini
   beans, drained and rinsed

Dressing
2 tbsp white wine vinegar
2 tsp Dijon mustard
4 tbsp olive oil
½ garlic clove, crushed
3 tbsp chopped parsley

Mary's tips

* *Salad can be assembled up to 6 hours ahead. Dressing can be made up to 3 days ahead. Dress just before serving.*

* *Not for freezing.*

Cook the broad beans in boiling salted water for 5 minutes. Drain and refresh under cold water, then slip the beans out their skins.

Cut the samphire in half and cook in boiling water for 2 minutes. Drain and refresh under cold water, then drain again.

Mix the broad beans, samphire and cannellini beans together in a bowl and season well with black pepper. Spoon into a serving dish.

Place all the dressing ingredients in a jug and whisk well.

Pour the dressing over the salad just before serving.

Squash, Feta and Spinach Salad

Serves 4–6

Bright and hearty, this salad will be a firm favourite. It is best to crumble
feta rather than cut it into cubes, and it is then creamier.

600g (1lb 5oz) peeled
butternut squash, cut
into 1cm (½in) cubes

2 tbsp olive oil

1 Romaine lettuce, sliced

75g (3oz) baby spinach
leaves, halved if large

½ large cucumber,
deseeded and cut into
1cm (½in) cubes

200g (7oz) feta cheese,
crumbled

50g (2oz) pumpkin
seeds, toasted

4 pink radishes, thinly sliced

**Mustard Creamy
Dressing**

1 tbsp Dijon mustard

3 tbsp white wine vinegar

8 tbsp sunflower oil

4 tbsp mayonnaise

½ garlic clove, crushed

Pinch of caster sugar

....

Mary's tips

* *Salad can be assembled
up to 4 hours ahead.
Dressing can be made up
to a day ahead. Dress
just before serving.*

* *Not for freezing.*

Preheat the oven to 220°C/200°C fan/Gas 7 and line a
baking sheet with non-stick baking paper.

Add the squash and oil to the prepared baking sheet and
season with salt and black pepper. Toss together then roast
in the oven for 30 minutes, or until lightly golden. Leave
to cool.

Place the lettuce, spinach, cucumber, feta, roasted squash and
pumpkin seeds in a wide serving bowl. Sprinkle with salt and
black pepper, and scatter the radish slices over the top.

Measure all the dressing ingredients into a jug and whisk
until smooth.

Pour the dressing over the salad to serve.

Quinoa, Pepper, Tomato and Basil Salad

Serves 4–6

Such a great dish to have in the fridge for lunch or as a side salad, as it is so versatile. The dressing is important when you serve quinoa, to give it flavour. I like using the red and white mixed quinoa, but you can use only white, if you prefer.

Salad

175g (6oz) red and white quinoa

¼ cucumber, deseeded and diced

2 celery sticks, diced

1 Romano pepper, deseeded and cut into thin, short strips

Small bunch of spring onions (about 6), sliced

Small bunch of basil, chopped

1 × 180g tub sun-blushed tomatoes in oil

Tomato Dressing

4 tbsp olive oil

2 tbsp white wine vinegar

1 tbsp grainy mustard

1 tsp honey

1 small garlic clove, crushed

2 tbsp sun-dried tomato paste

Mary's tips

* Can be made and dressed up to 24 hours ahead.

* Not for freezing.

* Be sure to season well.

Cook the quinoa in boiling water according to the packet instructions. Drain and leave to cool.

Measure the cucumber, celery, pepper, spring onions and basil into a large bowl. Drain the sun-dried tomatoes but reserve the oil. Chop the tomatoes and add to the bowl with the salad, then stir in the cooked quinoa. Season well with salt and black pepper.

To make the dressing, pour the reserved sun-blushed tomato oil into a jug and add the olive oil and vinegar. Measure the mustard, honey, garlic and sun-dried tomato paste into a small bowl and whisk well, then add the oils and vinegar, whisking again to combine.

Pour the dressing over the salad, toss to coat and serve.

Dill Pickled Vegetables

Makes 3 × 450g (1lb) jars

Wonderful to make when you have excess vegetables as pickling increases the shelf life. Pickling is an old preservation technique, but it is now popular and makes a lovely accompaniment to salads or to pep up a fish dish. Adding the salt in advance removes any bitter juices and excess liquid.

1 fennel bulb, sliced and chopped into 2cm (¾in) pieces

1 large red pepper, deseeded and chopped into 2cm (¾in) pieces

2 celery sticks, thinly sliced

300g (10½oz) cauliflower, broken into tiny florets

½ cucumber, halved lengthways, deseeded and thinly sliced

4 button shallots, halved (quartered if large)

15g (½oz) sea salt

Pickling Liquid

450ml (¾ pint) white wine vinegar

300g (10½oz) caster sugar

1 tbsp yellow mustard seeds

1 tbsp fresh or dried dill

1 tbsp whole black peppercorns

You will need 3 × 450g (1lb) jars.

....

Mary's tips

* *Can be made 1 month ahead. Once opened keep in the fridge.*

* *Not for freezing.*

Place all the vegetables in a large mixing bowl. Sprinkle with the salt and turn to coat. Leave for 3 hours.

Sterilise the jars by placing them in the sink and pouring boiling water over the top and inside. Leave for 30 minutes, then drain.

Rinse the vegetables in lots of cold water to remove the salt, then drain.

To make the pickling liquid, measure all the ingredients into a large pan and heat gently until dissolved. Increase the heat and boil for about 3 minutes. Reduce the heat and simmer for 5 minutes.

Divide the vegetables and pickling liquid between the jars. Seal while hot.

Preserved Lemons

Makes 1 × 700g (1lb 9oz) jar

I have had a lemon tree for 5 years and it produces lots of lemons – I use the misshapen ones for preserving. These are so easy to make and are wonderful to keep in the store cupboard for adding to stews and sauces (see page 52). They are a lovely gift in a jar with a ribbon, too. Clip-top jars are the best – a Kilner jar or similar.

About 150g (5oz) sea salt

5 unwaxed lemons, washed and quartered

You will need 1 × 700g (1lb 9oz) clip-top jar.

....

Mary's tips

* *Keeps for 3 months.*
* *Not for freezing.*
* *Over time, the lemons and salt will produce a brine. If there isn't enough brine to cover all the lemons, you can top up the jar with cold water and reseal.*

Sterilise the jar by placing it in the sink and pouring boiling water over the top and inside. Leave for 30 minutes, then drain.

Cover the base of the jar with a layer of salt. Add a layer of lemons, then sprinkle with more salt. Continue to layer the lemons and salt until you reach the top of the jar. Press the lemons down well into the jar. Seal the top and shake.

Place in a dark cupboard for 3 months, turning and shaking the jar daily (or whenever you remember!). The lemons will darken with storage.

Store in the fridge once opened.

PUDDINGS

Chocolate Profiteroles

Makes 12

Oh-so delicious and impressive, too. Choux pastry is not difficult to make if the recipe is followed carefully. It is important to add the sifted flour all at once, so the mixture does not become lumpy. When we were taught at college, we were told to 'shoot' the flour in, which explains it well. Piled in a wonderful pyramid and scattered with spun sugar, this simple bun becomes the celebrated wedding cake, croquembouche.

50g (2oz) butter

150ml (¼ pint) water

75g (3oz) plain flour, sifted

2 eggs, beaten, plus
   1 extra egg, beaten

200ml (⅓ pint) pouring
   double cream

Chocolate Sauce

75ml (2½fl oz) double cream

75g (3oz) Bournville
   dark chocolate,
   broken into pieces

Mary's tips

* Can be made and assembled
up to 4 hours ahead.
Unfilled buns can be made
up to a day ahead.

* Not for freezing.

Preheat the oven to 220°C/200°C fan/Gas 7 and line a baking sheet with non-stick baking paper.

Place the butter and water in a small saucepan over a high heat and cook until the water is boiling and the butter has melted. Remove from the heat and immediately shoot in the flour, all at once. Quickly beat with a wooden spoon until the mixture comes together and makes a smooth, thick dough. Add the beaten egg, a little at a time, beating after each addition, until the egg is incorporated and the dough is thick and smooth.

Spoon 12 domes of pastry on to the baking sheet. Brush with the extra beaten egg and bake for 10 minutes. Turn down the temperature to 190°C/170°C fan/Gas 5 and bake for another 20 minutes.

Remove the buns from the oven and turn the oven off. Slice each bun in half and put the buns cut side up back on to the baking sheet. Return to the oven for 15–20 minutes to dry out.

Meanwhile, to make the chocolate sauce, pour the cream into a pan and heat until hot. Add the chocolate and stir until melted. Remove from the heat and set aside in a cool place to thicken up.

Once the buns have dried out and are crisp, dip one half into the chocolate sauce and place on a wire rack to set. Repeat with 11 bun tops.

Pour the cream into a large bowl and whisk until it forms soft peaks. Place a generous dollop of whipped cream on to the remaining bun halves, then sandwich a chocolate half on top. Repeat to make 12 profiteroles.

White Chocolate and Biscoff Mousse

Serves 8

Biscoff biscuits are crispy caramel biscuits, now sold worldwide and easy to buy.
They are a perfect marriage with white chocolate and my husband loves them
with his coffee, too. The mousse is fairly rich, so serve it in small glasses or pots.
White chocolate can be tricky to melt, so buy a continental 100% white chocolate,
rather than a posh one, as these can overheat too quickly and not set.

100g (4oz) white chocolate,
broken into pieces

300ml (½ pint) pouring
double cream

1 egg white

25g (1oz) caster sugar

75g (3oz) full-fat
cream cheese

75g (3oz) Biscoff biscuits

....

Mary's tips

* *Do not overheat the
chocolate or it will split
the mousse.*

* *Can be made up to
6 hours ahead.*

* *Not for freezing.*

Place the white chocolate pieces in a small heatproof bowl
and pour in a third of the double cream. Sit the bowl over
a pan of just simmering water, taking care not to let the
water touch the base of the bowl, and heat gently, stirring
until the chocolate has melted. Set aside to cool and thicken
slightly in a cold place.

Meanwhile, lightly whisk the remaining cream until just
before it forms stiff peaks.

In a separate bowl, whisk the egg white until stiff. Add the
sugar a teaspoon at a time, whisking after each addition,
until shiny and glossy.

Measure the cream cheese into another mixing bowl and
beat until smooth (use an electric whisk to beat smooth,
if needed). Fold in the whipped cream, the white chocolate
mixture and finally the egg white. Fold lightly until
incorporated but be careful not to lose any air.

Place the biscuits in a bag and crush to fairly fine crumbs
with a rolling pin.

Divide half of the mousse between 8 little glasses. Sprinkle
half the biscuit crumbs on top, then repeat the layers with
the remaining mousse and crumbs. You should end up with
a layer of biscuit through the middle of the mousse and a
layer of biscuit on top.

Place in the fridge to chill for 1 hour before serving.

Crème Caramel

Serves 6

There is something so decadent and spoiling about crème caramel and yet it is pretty easy to make. We adore it and I like to make it often, as it can be finished a couple of days ahead. If you don't have full-fat milk, use 400ml (14fl oz) skimmed milk and 50ml (2fl oz) pouring double cream.

A knob of butter, to
  grease the ramekins
450ml (¾ pint) full-fat milk
3 large eggs
40g (1½oz) caster sugar
1 tsp vanilla extract

Caramel
175g (6oz) granulated sugar
150ml (¼ pint) water

You will need 6 × 150ml
  (¼ pint) size 1 ramekins.

Mary's tips

* Can be made up to
  2 days ahead.
* Not for freezing.
* Cooking gently in a
  bain marie prevents the
  custards from curdling.

Preheat the oven to 150°C/130°C fan/Gas 2.

To make the caramel, measure the sugar and water into a clean, stainless steel saucepan. Dissolve the sugar over a low heat, stirring gently with a wooden spoon until clear. Remove the spoon, increase the heat and boil the syrup until you have a golden-brown caramel. Quickly pour the caramel into the ramekins.

When the caramel is cool, lightly butter the sides of the ramekins, above the caramel. This will make the crème caramels easier to turn out.

Heat the milk in a saucepan until hand hot, then remove from the heat.

Break the eggs into a medium bowl and add the caster sugar and vanilla. Whisk, using an electric whisk, until combined. Gradually pour in the warm milk and continue to whisk until smooth. Pour through a sieve into a jug.

Line a small, high-sided roasting tin with kitchen paper and stand the ramekins on top. Carefully divide the custard between the dishes. Pour boiling water into the tin until it reaches halfway up the sides of the ramekins. Transfer the tin to the oven and cook for 40 minutes, until the custards are just set, with a slight wobble in the centre. Remove from the tin and leave to cool, then place in the fridge for 24 hours.

When ready to serve, gently loosen the custard away from the edges of the ramekins using your finger. Turn upside down on to a small plate. Remove the ramekin just before serving, allowing the caramel juices to run around the plate.

Elderflower and Limoncello Syllabub

Syllabub is a recipe which has been round for centuries. Once made by curdling sweet cream or milk with an acid, such as cider or wine, it has evolved into a creamy pudding made from wine, cream and lemon – I love this latest recipe of mine.

100ml (3½fl oz) elderflower cordial

3 tbsp Limoncello

Juice of 1 lemon

300ml (½ pint) pouring double cream

To decorate

Crystallised flowers or yellow raspberries and mint sprigs

Mary's tips

* *Can be made up to 8 hours ahead.*

* *Not for freezing.*

* *This dessert deserves to be served in beautiful, stemmed glasses to show it in all its glory.*

Measure the cordial, Limoncello and lemon juice into a large mixing bowl. Pour in the double cream and whisk using an electric whisk until soft peaks consistency.

Spoon into 6 glasses and place in the fridge to chill.

Top with crystallised flowers, raspberries and mint sprigs to serve.

Pink Meringue Kisses

Makes 60

These are tiny meringues, perfect for sandwiching together with cream or piling in a glass jar to give as a gift. Freeze-dried raspberries give a wonderful explosion of flavour.

4 large egg whites
225g (8oz) caster sugar
Pink food colouring gel
1 tbsp freeze-dried
   raspberries

....

Mary's tips

* *Can be made up to
   a month ahead.*

* *Freeze in a
   Tupperware box.*

* *If the meringue sticks to
   the baking paper slightly,
   it just means they need a
   little bit longer in the oven.*

Preheat the oven to 140°C/120°C fan/Gas 1. Line two large baking sheets with non-stick baking paper. Fit a piping bag with a plain nozzle.

To make the meringue, measure the egg whites into a large bowl and whisk with an electric whisk or in a mixer on full speed until stiff but not dry, like cloud. Gradually add the sugar, a little at a time, still whisking on full speed, until shiny and glossy.

Add 3 drops of pink colouring and the freeze-dried raspberries and stir gently to combine.

Spoon into the piping bag and pipe the meringue in tiny blobs on to the baking sheets. Bake in the oven for 35–40 minutes, or until they are just firm and come away easily from the baking sheet. After a few minutes, transfer carefully to a wire rack.

Serve in a bowl or on a platter with whipped cream and fresh fruit.

Lemon and Lime Meringue Tranche Pie

Serves 8–10

Such a favourite dessert for so many, the added lime gives it an extra zing. We have made this in a tranche tin but it would also fit in a deep 23cm (9in) round loose-bottomed flan tin.

Sweet Shortcrust Pastry
150g (5oz) plain flour
90g (3½oz) butter, cubed
2 tbsp icing sugar
1 egg

Filling
30g (1¼oz) cornflour
Finely grated zest and
   juice of 1 large lemon
Finely grated zest and
   juice of 1 large lime
50g (2oz) caster sugar
3 egg yolks

Meringue Topping
3 egg whites
175g (6oz) caster sugar

You will need a
   12 × 36 × 2.5cm
   (4½ × 14¼ × 1in)
   rectangular loose-
   bottomed fluted tin,
   or tranche tin.

Mary's tips

* *Can be made up to
   8 hours ahead and
   reheated gently to serve.*

* *Not for freezing.*

* *Do not serve the pie hot,
   as the filling may be a
   bit soft and will spill out
   of the pastry case.*

To make the pastry, measure the flour, butter and sugar into a food processor. Whiz until the mixture resembles fine breadcrumbs. Add the egg and whiz again until the dough comes together to form a ball. Turn out on to a lightly floured work surface and roll thinly. Carefully line the tin and press the pastry into the sides. Prick the base with a fork and place in the fridge to chill for 30 minutes.

Preheat the oven to 200°C/180°C fan/Gas 6 and place a baking tray in the oven to get very hot.

Line the pastry case with non-stick baking paper, add baking beans, place on the hot baking tray and bake for 15 minutes. Remove the beans and paper and bake for another 5 minutes, or until the pastry is crisp and lightly golden. Leave to cool. Reduce the oven temperature to 150°C/130°C fan/Gas 2.

To make the filling, measure the cornflour and 200ml (⅓ pint) water into a pan and whisk to combine. Add the zest and juice of the lemon and lime and place over a medium heat. Continue to whisk until the mixture has boiled and thickened. Remove from the heat, add the sugar and egg yolks and whisk again. Pour into the pastry case and place in the fridge to chill.

Meanwhile, make the meringue topping. Place the egg whites in a large bowl and whisk using an electric whisk, until stiff. Add the sugar a little at a time, whisking on full speed, until you have a shiny, glossy meringue. Spoon into a piping bag fitted with a plain 1½cm (⅝in) nozzle and pipe even blobs over the surface of the chilled custard in a neat pattern. If you don't have a piping bag, you can use two dessertspoons.

Bake in the oven for 35–40 minutes, until pale golden on top and firm to touch. Leave to cool in the tin for 15 minutes before removing from the tin. Serve warm with pouring cream.

Apricot Delice

Serves 4–6

A delicate yoghurt and apricot dessert – perfect for making ahead. Make in individual pots or glasses and serve chilled. Depending on the season, decorate with tiny mint leaves, borage flowers, which are a lovely vibrant blue, lemon verbena leaves, orange zest or edible flowers – anything to make it pretty and your eyes smile.

150g (5oz) dried apricots

200ml (⅓ pint) orange juice from a carton or freshly squeezed

25g (1oz) caster sugar

Juice of ½ small lemon

150ml (¼ pint) double cream

200g (7oz) natural yoghurt

Mint sprigs, finely grated orange zest or borage leaves, to decorate

Mary's tips

* *Can be made up to 8 hours ahead.*

* *Not for freezing.*

Place the apricots, orange juice, sugar and lemon juice in a saucepan. Cover with a lid and bring up to the boil, stirring occasionally until the sugar has dissolved. Reduce the heat and simmer gently for 30 minutes, until the apricots are very soft and most of the orange juice has been absorbed into the fruit.

Remove from the heat and blitz with a hand blender or tip into a processor and whiz until completely smooth without any lumps. Spoon into a bowl and set aside to cool.

Pour the cream into a large bowl and whisk until it forms soft peaks.

Add the yoghurt to the cold apricot purée, then fold in the whipped cream. Spoon into small glasses and place in the fridge to chill for 2 hours.

Garnish with mint sprigs, orange zest or borage leaves, depending on the time of year to serve.

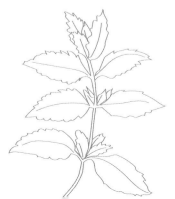

Lemon Limoncello Pavlova

Serves 8

This recipe comes from a chat with my friend Claudia Winkleman. We work together on the *Best Home Cook* TV show and have the most hilarious chats in between filming. When talking desserts, she said she would dream of lemon and meringue – so, Claud, this one is for you!

3 large egg whites

175g (6oz) caster sugar

1 tsp cornflour

1 tsp white wine vinegar

1 × 312g jar luxury
    lemon curd

450ml (¾ pint) double cream

150ml (¼ pint) crème fraîche

4 tbsp Limoncello

Finely grated zest of 1 lemon

....

Mary's tips

* *Pavlova can be made up to a month ahead. Carefully wrap in foil and keep on a shelf or freeze – no need to defrost before filling, so long as you fill 4 hours before serving.*

* *Freezes well but best not to as it can easily be damaged.*

* *If using a free-standing electric mixer on full speed, you can add the sugar in dessertspoonfuls, which makes the process a little quicker.*

Preheat the oven to 160°C/140°C fan/Gas 3 and line a baking sheet with non-stick baking paper.

Place the egg whites in a large bowl. Whisk using an electric whisk on full speed until stiff but not dry, like cloud. Gradually add the sugar, a little at a time, still whisking at full speed, until shiny and glossy. The meringue should hold its shape in peaks.

Mix the cornflour and vinegar together in a small bowl. Stir carefully into the meringue.

Spoon the meringue on to the baking sheet and use the back of a spoon to spread it out to make a rough circle measuring about 23cm (9in) in diameter. Arrange the meringue so that it dips slightly in the centre and is raised slightly around the sides. Bake for about 1 hour, or until firm to touch. Turn off the oven and leave to dry out inside the oven for another hour. Finally, remove from the oven and set aside.

Using half of the curd, spread a layer over the base of the pavlova.

Pour the cream into a large bowl and whisk using an electric whisk until soft peaks. Stir in the crème fraîche and Limoncello, then swirl in the remaining lemon curd. Spread the cream mixture on top of the lemon curd.

Sprinkle with grated lemon zest to serve.

Lime Posset

Serves 8

I usually make lemon posset with double cream but for a change we have used crème fraîche and lime. There is a lovely sharpness to it, and it is a fraction less fattening than a posset made with double cream. Expect it to be slightly less set, though.

500g (1lb 2oz) full-fat crème fraîche

80g (3oz) caster sugar

Finely grated zest and juice of 3 limes

1 slice of lime, cut into 8 pieces

You will need 8 small glasses or ramekins.

Mary's tips

* *You must use full-fat crème fraîche; the light version will not set the posset.*
* *Can be made up to a day ahead.*
* *Not for freezing.*

Place the crème fraîche, sugar and lime zest in a saucepan. Heat until just below simmering point and the sugar has dissolved. Remove from the heat and leave for a few minutes.

Pour in the lime juice and stir. Allow to thicken slightly.

Pour into the glasses or ramekins and place in the fridge to chill for 6 hours, or ideally overnight, until set.

Place a small piece of lime on top of each posset before serving.

Blood Orange Sorbet

Serves 6

There is a strange misconception that sorbet is healthier than ice cream. In fact, while sorbet may have no fat, it does have lots of sugar, so go steady on the portion size. Ice cream does have less sugar, but it has cream, so more fat! Whichever you choose, they are both naughty but delicious!

600ml (1 pint) blood orange juice from a carton
200g (7oz) caster sugar

You will need a 900g (2lb) plastic container.

Mary's tips

* *Freeze for up to 4 months.*
* *To make Passionfruit Sorbet, replace the orange juice with passionfruit juice from a carton.*
* *The whizzing in the processor breaks up the crystals and gives a smooth sorbet.*

Measure the orange juice and sugar into a saucepan. Stir over a medium heat until the sugar has dissolved.

Pour into the plastic container, cover and freeze for 4–6 hours until frozen.

Slice the frozen mixture into pieces and place in a food processor. Whiz until the mixture looks slushy but not liquid. Return to the container and smooth with the back of a spoon. Freeze for another 4 hours until frozen.

Scoop into balls to serve.

Chocolate Chip Ice Cream

Makes about 675g (1 ½ l b)

An inexpensive simple ice cream made from cocoa powder and
evaporated milk – this is one the kids will adore.

1 × 410g tin evaporated milk
3 tbsp cocoa powder
4 tbsp boiling water
300ml (½ pint) double cream
100g (4oz) icing sugar, sifted
100g (4oz) small milk
   chocolate chips

You will need a 900g
   (2lb) plastic container.

Mary's tip

* *Freeze for up to 3 months.*

Place the evaporated milk in the fridge for 1–2 hours
to chill.

Sift the cocoa powder into a bowl. Add the boiling water
and mix to a smooth paste. Leave to cool slightly.

Pour the double cream into a large bowl and whisk with an
electric whisk until soft peaks. Fold in the chocolate mixture
and the icing sugar.

Pour the chilled evaporated milk into the bowl of a mixer
and whisk on maximum speed until whipped cream
consistency and it has doubled in volume. This will take
4–5 minutes.

Fold the whipped milk into the chocolate cream mixture,
then carefully stir in the chocolate chips.

Pour into the plastic container and transfer to the freezer
for a minimum of 6 hours or overnight.

Scoop into balls to serve.

Tiramisu Ice Cream

Makes about 675g (1 ½ lb)

Made with coffee, brandy and mascarpone, this is the ultimate tiramisu ice cream. Adding the condensed milk gives a little extra sweetness.

250g (9oz) mascarpone
   cheese
300ml (½ pint) double cream
1 × 397g tin condensed milk
1 tsp vanilla extract
1 tbsp cocoa powder
1 tbsp strong instant coffee
   powder (espresso is best)
3 tbsp boiling water
3 tbsp brandy
50g (2oz) Bournville dark
   chocolate, finely chopped

You will need a 900g
   (2lb) plastic container.

....

Mary's tip

* *Freeze for up to 3 months.*

Measure the mascarpone into a bowl. Beat using a wooden spoon until it has loosened. Add the cream and whisk using an electric whisk until it forms soft peaks. Whisk in the condensed milk and vanilla, then divide between two bowls.

Measure the cocoa powder and coffee powder into a small bowl. Add the boiling water and stir to dissolve. Stir in the brandy and allow to cool.

Add the chocolate coffee mixture to one bowl of cream and stir until smooth.

Spoon both mixtures into the container, gently stirring to give a ripple effect. Sprinkle the chocolate on top. Cover and freeze for 12 hours.

Scoop into balls to serve.

Mint Choc Chip Ice Cream

Makes about 675g (1 ½ lb)

Be sure to buy natural colourings and flavourings. Peppermint extract comes
straight from the plant, whereas essence is manufactured artificially.

4 eggs, separated

300ml (½ pint) double cream

1 dessertspoon green
food gel colouring

1½ tsp peppermint extract

100g (4oz) caster sugar

200g (7oz) dark
chocolate chips

You will need a 900g
(2lb) plastic container.

....

Mary's tip

* *Freeze for up to 3 months.*

Place the egg yolks in a small bowl and use a fork to beat
until just combined.

Measure the cream into a large bowl. Add the food
colouring and whisk, using an electric whisk, until soft
peaks. Stir in the peppermint extract and the egg yolks.

Place the egg whites in a large clean bowl. Whisk using an
electric whisk until stiff like cloud. Add the sugar a little at a
time, still whisking on maximum speed, until stiff and glossy.

Add a little of the whisked egg whites to the cream to
slacken the mixture, then carefully fold in the remaining
whites until incorporated. Take care not to knock out any
air from the whisked egg whites.

Stir in the chocolate chips and spoon into the plastic
container. Freeze for a minimum of 8 hours.

Scoop into balls to serve.

Toffee Fudge Ice Cream

Makes 900g (2lb)

Double toffee and so very moreish. Delicious served with the Poached Pears with Apple and Cinnamon on page 243 or the Pear and Almond Tart on page 244. Tins of caramel are easy to buy and save you the trouble of boiling the tin of condensed milk to achieve the toffee flavour. I am not keen on salted caramel, but I know it is popular so, if liked, you could add chunks of salted caramel fudge.

450ml (¾ pint) double cream

1 × 397g tin caramel
   condensed milk

2 large eggs, separated

1 tsp vanilla extract

100g (4oz) caster sugar

75g (3oz) fudge, cut
   into small cubes

You will need a 900g
   (2lb) plastic container.

....

Mary's tip

* *Freeze for up to 3 months.*

Measure the double cream into a large bowl. Whisk with an electric whisk until it forms soft peaks. Add the caramel and gently, on a low speed, continue to whisk until smooth.

Place the yolks in a small bowl and beat until light. Stir into the cream with the vanilla.

Place the egg whites in a large clean bowl. Whisk using an electric whisk until stiff like cloud. Add the sugar a little at a time, still whisking on maximum speed, until shiny and glossy.

Fold the cream and fudge chunks into the egg whites carefully to combine.

Spoon into the container and freeze for a minimum of 12 hours.

Remove from the freezer for 5 minutes before serving. Scoop into balls to serve.

Frozen Berry Yoghurt

Serves 6

Just as delicious as ice cream, this is a joy to keep in the freezer.
Keep in a tub or in pre-scooped balls for easy serving. You can make
this with frozen berries, too; just defrost before whizzing.

350g (12oz) mixed berries
(e.g. raspberries,
blueberries and
strawberries)
150ml (¼ pint) double cream
500g (1lb 2oz) full-fat
natural yoghurt
100g (4oz) runny honey
1 tsp vanilla extract

You will need a 1.2
litre (2 pint) shallow
plastic container.

Mary's tips

* *Freeze for up to a month.*
* *Whizzing the frozen
mixture removes the ice
crystals and gives a smooth,
luxurious yoghurt ice cream.*

Tip all the berries into a food processor. Whiz until you
have a coulis consistency.

Pour the cream into a large bowl and whisk until it forms
soft peaks. Add the yoghurt, honey, vanilla and berries,
and fold together until combined.

Spoon into the plastic container and freeze for about
6 hours, or until frozen.

Slice the frozen fruity yoghurt into pieces and place in a
food processor. Whiz until the mixture looks slushy but
not liquid. Return to the container and freeze for another
4 hours until frozen.

Scoop into balls to serve.

Five Smoothies

Serves 2

I know the young love smoothies and I suppose when I was younger a milkshake was a similar treat. These are much healthier than an ice-cream-laden milkshake, of course!

Mango and Passionfruit

5 passionfruit, seeds and
  juice scooped out
50g (2oz) ripe banana, sliced
50g (2oz) ripe peeled mango, sliced
50ml (2fl oz) oat milk
75ml (3fl oz) pineapple juice

Pineapple and Coconut

75g (3oz) fresh peeled pineapple, sliced
100g (4oz) ripe banana, sliced
100ml (3½fl oz) coconut milk
100ml (3½fl oz) pineapple juice

Healthy Green

25g (1oz) baby spinach
30g (1¼oz) peeled avocado, sliced
75g (3oz) fresh peeled pineapple, sliced
30g (1¼oz) peeled kiwi, sliced
½ tsp chia seeds
150ml (¼ pint) orange juice
A squeeze of lime juice

Strawberry, Oat and Yoghurt

150g (5oz) strawberries
50g (2oz) natural yoghurt
1 tsp honey
300ml (½ pint) oat milk

Breakfast Blueberry and Oat

75g (3oz) ripe banana, sliced
2 tsp honey
1 tbsp porridge oats
100g (4oz) blueberries
150ml (¼ pint) oat milk

....

Measure all the ingredients into a blender and whiz until smooth.

Pour into glasses to serve.

....

Mary's tips

* *Freeze prepared fruit in a bag to prepare ahead. Use from frozen.*

For the Love of ... Fruit

Summer Fruits

I love all the soft fruits as they come
into season, one after the other from
June. First to arrive are the strawberries,
followed by raspberries and gooseberries.
Pick gooseberries green for pies and
crumbles, or fully ripe for eating raw.
One of my favourite ways to eat berries
is simply in a bowl with cream, but
we've tried something different with our
Frozen Berry Yoghurt (see page 232).
Blueberries add wonderful colour, as
well as flavour, to a bake (see page 253),
and they freeze well. Blackcurrants
and redcurrants freeze well, too, but
it's best to pick them from the stalks
first. I always have a jar of homemade
redcurrant jelly on the shelf.

Apples, Pears and Plums

I don't think you can beat a Bramley
apple for cooking, but there is such a
huge variety of apples available now, and
it is wonderful to see. The young like a
sweet dessert apple, and Pink Lady is
usually their first choice. If I'm poaching
apples (see page 240), I would choose a
dessert variety and find that Braeburns
work well. Pears are best to let ripen
at home, if you are buying them, and
William or Conference seem to be the
most reliable varieties. They both have
great flavour. Victoria plums are my
favourite – naturally sweet and thick
skinned, they are good for eating raw
or cooking.

Lemons and Limes

Always buy unwaxed lemons – otherwise, when you use the zest so much of what you are adding to a bake is wax! Warming them in a bowl of very hot water or placing them in the microwave for a few moments will make them easier to squeeze. We grow lemons at home with great success. We bring the potted tree inside the greenhouse for winter and place it out in a sunny spot in the summer. They need some feeding in the growing season but we always get an abundance of fruit.

Tomatoes

Flavour is of paramount importance with tomatoes. Some of the industrial varieties can be completely bland, so beware. Deep red Piccolo and yellow Sungold tomatoes are first rate for taste if you buy them on the vine. There is such a wonderful variety of Heritage tomatoes, too, of various colours – some are even striped – and they can give wonderful interest to a tomato salad. If you're growing tomatoes at home, try Gardener's Delight.

Avocado

Also known around the world as Alligator Pear or Butter Fruit, avocados are such a favourite of mine. Ripen them at home wrapped in newspaper and press near the stem to test if they are ripe – it should be gently soft. There is a round stone in the middle of the fruit, so cut around it. The flesh will discolour once sliced, so to prevent this, squeeze lemon juice over the surface and it won't turn black.

Boozy Fruits with Port

Serves 6

Wonderful in colour and using all the autumnal fruits we grow at home or buy in season when they are at their finest. Buying in season is so important to me. I remember waiting for the blackberry season as a child – it was such an excitement and I still try and buy in season, so the fruit and vegetables are tasting at their finest. This is ideal as a dessert or for breakfast.

25g (1oz) butter

2 dessert apples, peeled, cored and thickly sliced

50g (2oz) caster sugar

100ml (3½fl oz) Port

2 just-ripe pears, peeled, cored and thickly sliced

6 plums, stoned and each cut into 8 pieces

2 figs, each cut into quarters

150g (5oz) blackberries

....

Mary's tips

* *Can be made up to 8 hours ahead.*

* *Freezes well.*

Place the butter in a wide-based pan over a medium heat until melted. Add the apples and stir over the heat for 2 minutes.

Sprinkle in the sugar and pour in the Port. Bring up to the boil, stirring, until the sugar has dissolved.

Add the pears, plums and figs, and simmer with the lid on for about 5 minutes, or until the figs are tender. Remove from the heat and add the blackberries. Leave to cool.

Serve chilled with low-fat crème fraîche.

Poached Pears
with Apple and Cinnamon

Serves 6

I love puds that can be made ahead for when friends are coming round.
Serve this as a fresh alternative to another creamy indulgent pudding!

1 litre (1¾ pints) apple juice

150g (5oz) caster sugar

Finely grated zest and
juice of ½ lemon

2 cinnamon sticks

6 ripe but firm pears

....

Mary's tips

* *Can be made up to
6 hours ahead.*

* *Not for freezing.*

Measure the apple juice, half the sugar, the lemon zest and juice and the cinnamon sticks into a deep saucepan. Bring up to the boil, stirring so the sugar dissolves.

Peel and halve the pears lengthways through the stem. Carefully scoop out the core using a ½ teaspoon or small knife. Add the pears to the poaching liquid, cover with a lid and simmer gently for about 15 minutes, or until tender.

Remove from the heat and leave to cool slightly in the poaching liquid for 15 minutes.

Spoon the pears into a serving bowl. Add the remaining sugar to the liquid in the pan and bring to the boil. Let the liquid reduce over a high heat until it has a slightly syrupy consistency and has reduced to about 500ml (¾ pint). Pour over the pears and leave to cool completely.

Serve at room temperature with crème fraîche.

Pear and Almond Tart

Serves 8

One of my favourite flavour combinations, this tart is so impressive for when guests are visiting. Quick to make and great as it can be made ahead and reheated.

2 × 400g tins pears, cut into quarters

Sweet Pastry

175g (6oz) plain flour

75g (3oz) butter

1 tbsp icing sugar

1 egg

1 tbsp water

Almond Filling

100g (4oz) butter

100g (4oz) caster sugar

4 eggs

100g (4oz) ground almonds

1 tsp almond extract

50g (2oz) plain flour

Topping

25g (1oz) icing sugar

About 2 tbsp fresh lemon juice

25g (1oz) flaked almonds, toasted

You will need a deep 28cm (11in) loose-bottomed fluted flan tin.

Mary's tips

* *Can be made up to a day ahead and reheated to serve.*

* *Freezes well cooked.*

To make the pastry, measure the flour, butter and icing sugar into a food processor. Whiz until the mixture resembles breadcrumbs. Add the egg and water and whiz again until the dough comes together to form a ball.

Sprinkle a worktop with flour and roll the pastry out until it is 3cm (1¼in) bigger than the base of the tin. Carefully transfer to the tin and line the base and sides. Press into the sides and make a lip around the top edge. Prick the base with a fork and place in the fridge to chill for 30 minutes.

Preheat the oven to 200°C/180°C fan/Gas 6.

Line the pastry case with non-stick baking paper and fill with baking beans. Bake blind in the oven for 15 minutes, then remove the paper and beans and return to the oven for a further 5 minutes, until lightly golden.

Meanwhile, make the filling by creaming the butter and sugar together in a food processor. Add the eggs, ground almonds, extract and flour and whiz again until smooth.

Pour the filling into the pastry case. Arrange the pears on top, scattered or in a spiral, and bake for about 30 minutes, or until golden brown and just set in the middle. Set aside to cool in the tin for a few minutes.

Mix the icing sugar and lemon juice together in a small bowl to make a runny icing. Drizzle over the tart and scatter with the flaked almonds.

Remove from the tin and serve warm in wedges with crème fraîche.

Lumpy Bumpy Plum Pie

Serves 6–8

Using plums straight from the tree, this is an easy early autumn pie. I prefer Victoria plums as they have the best flavour and colour when cooked. Choose a round ovenproof dish that is not too deep and roll the pastry thinly, so it cooks evenly. The pastry has icing sugar added, which helps it to mould over the plums to give the bumpy shapes.

25g (1oz) cornflour

100g (4oz) caster sugar

900g (2lb) plums,
  halved and stoned

1 egg, beaten

Shortcrust Pastry

225g (8oz) plain flour

75g (3oz) icing sugar

100g (4oz) butter, diced

1 egg, beaten

You will need a 28cm
  (11in) shallow, round
  ovenproof dish.

Mary's tips

* *Can be made up to 8 hours ahead and reheated.*

* *Freezes well raw or cooked.*

* *When laying the top pastry on top, do not stretch it but let it rest gently on the plums and mould over them. Tucking the pastry in allows for movement and a little shrinkage.*

To make the pastry, measure the flour, icing sugar and butter into a food processor. Whiz until the mixture resembles breadcrumbs. Add the egg and whiz again until the pastry just comes together (it will be a soft dough). Shape into a ball, wrap in cling film and place in the fridge to chill for 30 minutes.

Preheat the oven to 200°C/180°C fan/Gas 6.

Place the cornflour and sugar in a bowl and mix. Arrange the plums cut side down in the dish and sprinkle the cornflour and sugar mixture over the top.

Roll out the chilled pastry fairly thinly and trim to a neat round about 2cm (¾in) bigger than the dish. Carefully lift the pastry and place over the plums, loosely tucking in the edges. Brush the top of the pie with the beaten egg and bake in the oven for 40–45 minutes, until lightly golden.

Leave to cool slightly before serving with custard, cream, crème fraîche or ice cream!

Passionfruit Tart with Orange Pastry

Serves 6–8

Think tarte au citron but with passionfruit – completely divine! Gentle cooking ensures the filling is smooth and creamy, so be careful not to let it bubble. Baking the pastry blind ensures it is completely cooked underneath.

8 passionfruit

4 large eggs

Juice of 1 large orange (or 50ml/2 fl oz orange juice)

150ml (¼ pint) double cream

75g (3oz) caster sugar

Icing sugar, to dust

Orange Pastry

175g (6oz) plain flour

100g (4oz) cold butter, diced

30g (1¼oz) icing sugar

Finely grated zest of 1 orange

1 egg, beaten

You will need a deep 23cm (9in) loose-bottomed fluted tart tin.

Mary's tips

* *Can be made up to a day ahead.*

* *Freezes well.*

To make the orange pastry, measure the flour, butter, icing sugar and orange zest into a food processor. Whiz until the mixture resembles breadcrumbs. Add the egg and whiz again until the dough comes together to form a ball.

Sprinkle a work surface with flour and gently roll out the pastry until it is very thin. Carefully transfer to the tin and line the base and sides. Press into the sides of the fluted edges and level the top. Prick the base with a fork and place in the fridge to chill for a minimum of 30 minutes.

Preheat the oven to 200°C/180°C fan/Gas 6.

Line the pastry case with non-stick baking paper and fill with baking beans. Blind bake in the oven for about 15 minutes, or until lightly golden at the edges. Remove the paper and beans and return to the oven for a further 5 minutes, until the pastry is crisp and lightly golden.

Reduce the oven temperature to 160°C/140°C fan/Gas 3.

Slice the passionfruit in half and remove the pulp. Sieve the pulp into a large bowl, discarding the seeds. Break the eggs into the bowl, then add the orange juice, double cream and sugar, and beat well until combined.

Transfer the passionfruit custard into a jug, then pour into the pastry case and carefully slide back into the oven. Bake for 35–40 minutes, until the custard is just set in the middle with a very slight wobble.

Leave to cool, then place in the fridge to chill. Dust with icing sugar and serve at room temperature with cream on the side.

Apple and Cinnamon Dessert Cake

Serves 6–8

Think of a traditional sponge with fruit that your granny may
have made – this is similar complete comfort food.

225g (8oz) self-raising flour

1 level tsp baking powder

175g (6oz) caster sugar

2 eggs

1 tsp ground cinnamon

150g (5oz) butter, melted,
  plus extra for greasing

350g (12oz) cooking apples,
  peeled, cored and sliced

25g (1oz) flaked almonds

You will need a deep
  20cm (8in) loose-
  bottomed cake tin.

Mary's tips

* *Keep the piled apple slices
  in the centre, not around the
  edge, otherwise it will stick.*

* *Can be made up to 2 days
  ahead and reheated.*

* *Freezes well cooked.*

Preheat the oven to 160°C/140°C fan/Gas 3 and lightly grease
and base line the cake tin.

Measure the flour, baking powder, caster sugar, eggs,
ground cinnamon and butter into a bowl. Whisk using
an electric whisk until well blended.

Spoon half of the mixture into the base of the tin and
level the surface. Arrange the apples on top, piling them
mostly towards the centre. Using two dessertspoons, spoon
the remaining mixture on top and spread out to cover the
surface. Sprinkle with the flaked almonds. Bake in the oven
for 1¼–1½ hours, or until well risen, lightly golden and
coming away from the sides of the tin. Leave to cool in the
tin for 10 minutes.

Run a palette knife around the edge and remove from the
tin to cool completely.

Serve with cream or crème fraîche.

Sunday Lunch Apple and Blueberry Pudding

Makes 12 squares

Easy to make in a traybake tin and perfect for using up the windfall apples. Cut into squares and serve warm with custard or cream. You can use soft butter for this recipe, if preferred, but I think it works best with baking spread.

225g (8oz) baking spread, from the fridge, plus extra for greasing

225g (8oz) caster sugar

4 large eggs

2 tsp vanilla extract

2 tsp baking powder

350g (12oz) self-raising flour

350g (12oz) Bramley apples, peeled, cored and cut into fairly thin slices

200g (7oz) blueberries

Demerara sugar, to sprinkle

Mary's tips

* Can be made up to a day ahead and reheated to serve.

* Freezes well cooked.

Preheat the oven to 180°C/160°C fan/Gas 4 and grease a 23 × 30cm (9 × 12in) traybake tin.

Measure the baking spread, caster sugar, eggs, vanilla extract, baking powder and flour into a bowl. Whisk with an electric whisk until combined and light and creamy.

Spread half of the mixture into the base of the tin. Arrange half of the apples and half the blueberries on top in a mixed layer. Spread the remaining cake mixture over the top, then finish with the remaining apples and blueberries. Sprinkle with the demerara sugar and bake in the oven for 45–55 minutes, or until well risen and lightly golden brown.

Slice into squares to serve warm or cold.

BAKING

Melt-in-the-Mouth
Walnut Cheese Biscuits

Makes 20

These biscuits are a sort of savoury shortbread and are so moreish! If you see broken walnuts on the shelf when you are buying them, be sure to get them as they are cheaper and they taste the same! You could also use a different nut, if you prefer. These make a lovely gift, presented in a sustainable bamboo box, and are perfect to take when visiting friends.

75g (3oz) butter, diced

30g (1¼oz) semolina

50g (2oz) self-raising flour

50g (2oz) Parmesan,
   finely grated

1 tsp mustard powder

15g (½oz) walnuts,
   finely chopped

1½ tbsp beaten egg white

15g (½oz) poppy seeds

....

Mary's tips

* *Can be made up to
   4 days ahead and kept in
   an airtight tin lined with
   kitchen paper – this
   prevents the biscuits
   from becoming soggy.*

* *Freeze well. Refresh in a
   low oven after defrosting.*

Measure all the ingredients except the poppy seeds into a food processor. Season with salt and black pepper and whiz until well combined to a soft dough.

Turn the dough out on to a lightly floured work surface and roll into a cigar shape about 12cm (4½in) long and 4cm (1½in) wide.

Sprinkle the poppy seeds on to a board. Roll the dough in the seeds so the roll is completely covered. Carefully wrap in cling film and place in the freezer to chill for 30 minutes.

Preheat the oven to 200°C/180°C fan/Gas 6. Line a baking sheet with non-stick baking paper.

Slice the roll into 20 thin slices and arrange on the baking sheet. Bake in the oven for about 15 minutes, or until pale golden and just firm in the centre. Remove from the oven and leave to cool on the baking sheet for 5 minutes, then transfer to a wire rack to cool completely.

Nordic Seed and Nut Loaf

Makes 1 × 900g (2lb) loaf

This feels so healthy and is gluten free. Chia seeds are an edible seed from a plant native to Mexico and related to the mint family. They are very high in fibre and have health benefits. This recipe was inspired by food chats with my very lovely agent Joanna Kaye. In lockdown, phone chats about lunch were imperative! Joanna had eaten a delicious sounding seeded bread, and from that chat this recipe grew – we all love it! Swap the dates for cranberries or figs, if liked, using the same amount. A delicious combination of close firm texture and nutty flavour, this is great spread with butter and served with gravadlax or smoked salmon, charcuterie, cheese and pickles, or as a base for canapés.

Butter or oil, for greasing

4 large eggs

3 tbsp olive oil

50g (2oz) soft dried dates, finely chopped

¼ tsp sea salt

75g (3oz) pumpkin seeds

75g (3oz) sunflower seeds

150g (5oz) pecan nuts, finely chopped

50g (2oz) sesame seeds

3 tbsp chia seeds

....

Mary's tips

* Can be made up to a day before.

* Freezes well.

Preheat the oven to 180°C/160°C fan/Gas 4. Grease the base and sides of a 900g (2lb) loaf tin and line with non-stick baking paper.

Break the eggs into a bowl and beat with a fork until combined. Add the remaining ingredients and mix well using a wooden spoon.

Pour the mixture into the loaf tin and bake for 45–50 minutes, until golden brown and firm in the centre.

Leave to cool in the tin for 5 minutes, then loosen the edges with a palette knife, remove from the tin and place on a wire rack to cool completely.

Slice into thin slices to serve.

Crackle Cheese Biscuits

Makes 30

These are so moreish – great to have in the cupboard for when friends pop in.

100g (4oz) butter, softened
100g (4oz) plain flour
¼ tsp salt
100g (4oz) mature
    Cheddar, grated
25g (1oz) Rice Krispies

....

Mary's tips

* *Can be made up to
    a week ahead.*
* *Not for freezing.*

Preheat the oven to 180°C/160°C fan/Gas 4 and line two large baking sheets with non-stick baking paper.

Measure the butter, flour, salt and Cheddar into a food processor. Whiz until the mixture comes together. Spoon into a bowl and add the Rice Krispies. Mix well with your hands to combine.

Shape into 30 small balls. Place on the baking sheets and press down firmly with a fork. Bake in the oven for 18–20 minutes, until lightly golden.

Transfer to a wire rack and leave to cool.

Serve as a savoury snack to go with drinks.

Australian Banana Maple
and Date Loaf

Makes 1 × 900g (2lb) loaf

This is an Australian banana bread which is often served for breakfast and toasted, buttered and spread with maple syrup. Take care to add only a level teaspoon of bicarb, otherwise the loaf will taste a little bitter.

Butter or oil, for greasing

250g (9oz) overripe bananas (about 4), mashed

225g (8oz) light muscovado sugar

1 tsp vanilla extract

2 large eggs

60ml (2fl oz) maple syrup

½ tsp baking powder

1 tsp bicarbonate of soda

1 tsp ground cinnamon

250g (9oz) self-raising flour

50g (2oz) dates, pitted and finely chopped

....

Mary's tips

* *Can be made up to 2 days ahead.*

* *Freezes well.*

Preheat the oven to 180°C/160°C fan/Gas 4. Grease the base and sides of a 900g (2lb) loaf tin and line with a long strip of non-stick baking paper, covering the two long sides and the base.

Measure all the ingredients into a bowl. Whisk until light and fluffy with an electric whisk or using a free-standing mixer.

Spoon into the loaf tin and level the surface. Bake in the oven for about 1 hour, or until well risen and lightly golden.

Leave to cool in the tin for about 15 minutes, then run a palette knife along the short ends and turn out of the tin. Leave to cool completely on a wire rack.

Slice and served toasted with butter.

Lemon Poppy Seed Loaf Cakes

Makes 2 loaves

This is still one of my favourite cakes and making it in two loaf tins means you can make one and freeze the other for another day. I find it more successful when I use two 450g (1lb) loaf tins, rather than one 900g (2lb) tin. You may need to be flexible with the timings, as loaf tins come in slightly different shapes – if they are wider or deeper, the cakes may take a little longer to bake.

225g (8oz) baking spread, straight from the fridge, plus extra for greasing

225g (8oz) caster sugar

225g (8oz) self-raising flour

4 large eggs

1 tsp baking powder

Finely grated zest of 3 large lemons

1 tbsp poppy seeds

Icing

175g (6oz) icing sugar

Juice of ½ lemon

1 tbsp poppy seeds

....

Mary's tips

* *Can be made up to 2 days ahead.*

* *Freeze well un-iced.*

Preheat the oven to 180°C/160°C fan/Gas 4. Grease the base and sides of 2 × 450g (1lb) loaf tins and line with non-stick baking paper.

Measure all the loaf cake ingredients into a bowl and whisk together until light and fluffy, using an electric whisk or a free-standing mixer.

Divide the mixture between the tins and level the tops. Bake in the oven for 40–45 minutes, or until well risen and coming away from the side of the tins.

Leave to cool in the tins for 10 minutes, then carefully transfer to a wire rack to cool completely.

To make the icing, place the icing sugar in a small bowl and add enough lemon juice to make a thick icing. Spoon into a piping bag and snip off a small point. Pipe zig zags over the tops of the cakes and sprinkle with the poppy seeds. If you are in a hurry, spoon the icing on instead.

Leave to set for 10 minutes before cutting into thick slices to serve.

Madeira Cake

Serves 8

One of my favourite cakes, plain and simple with no icing but an irresistible old-fashioned cake at any time of day. This is traditionally topped with a slice of candied peel but if none is available, leave the top plain.

175g (6oz) softened butter, plus extra for greasing

175g (6oz) caster sugar

175g (6oz) self-raising flour

50g (2oz) ground almonds

4 large eggs

Finely grated zest of 1 lemon

Thin slices of candied lemon peel, to garnish

....

Mary's tips

* *Keeps for a week in an airtight tin.*

* *Freezes well cooked.*

Preheat the oven to 160°C/140°C fan/Gas 3. Grease and base line an 18cm (7in) deep round cake tin.

Measure all the ingredients, except the candied peel, into a large mixing bowl. Whisk together using an electric whisk until thoroughly mixed.

Spoon into the tin and level the top. Bake in the oven for 1½ hours, or until well risen and lightly golden. Insert a skewer into the centre of the cake to make sure it is cooked all the way through.

Place the slices of candied peel in the centre of the cake and leave to cool in the tin for 10 minutes, then turn out on to a wire rack to cool completely.

The Best Ginger Biscuits

Makes 16

You know your favourite crisp, thick, moreish ginger biscuit?
Well, this is it! Restraint is needed to keep the lid on the tin.

50g (2oz) butter

1 level tbsp golden syrup

175g (6oz) self-raising flour

1 level tbsp ground ginger

75g (3oz) crystallised
ginger, finely chopped

1 tsp bicarbonate of soda

50g (2oz) demerara sugar

50g (2oz) light
muscovado sugar

1 medium egg, beaten

....

Mary's tips

* *Keep well in an airtight
tin for 5 days.*

* *Freeze well. Refresh in a
low oven once defrosted.*

Preheat the oven to 160°C/140°C fan/Gas 3. Line two baking sheets with non-stick baking paper.

Measure the butter and golden syrup into a saucepan. Heat gently, stirring, until melted.

Place the flour, ground ginger, chopped ginger, bicarb and demerara and muscovado sugars in a mixing bowl. Mix well, then stir in the melted ingredients. Add the egg and bring the mixture together to form a dough.

Divide into 16 equal pieces and roll with your hands into small balls. Place on the baking sheets and slightly flatten to about 1cm (½in) thick. Bake for about 25 minutes, until golden and firm around the edges.

Leave to firm up on the baking sheets for a few minutes, then transfer to a wire rack to cool completely.

Chocolate Heart Biscuits

Makes about 25

These are adorable, simple chocolate biscuits, similar to an old-fashioned fork biscuit.

100g (4oz) butter, softened
50g (2oz) caster sugar
1 egg yolk
125g (4½oz) self-raising flour
25g (1oz) cocoa
    powder, sifted
Icing sugar, to dust

....

Mary's tips

* *These keep well in an airtight container for up to 3 weeks.*
* *Freeze well.*
* *When storing biscuits in the tin or the freezer, line the base and in between each layer of biscuits with kitchen paper; this prevents them from becoming soggy. If freezing, defrost and refresh in a moderate oven for a few minutes.*

Preheat the oven to 180°C/160°C fan/Gas 4. You will need a 5cm (2in) heart-shaped cutter. Line two baking sheets with non-stick baking paper.

Measure the butter and sugar into a large bowl. Whisk using an electric whisk, until fluffy. Add the egg yolk and whisk again to combine.

Add the flour and cocoa powder to the bowl, a tablespoon at a time, and continue to whisk until the mixture comes together and is all one colour.

Sprinkle a work surface with flour and roll out the dough to about 0.5cm (¼in) thick. Stamp out heart shapes using the cutter and place on the baking sheets. Re-roll the dough until you have 25 biscuits. Bake for about 12 minutes, until just firm to touch.

Leave to cool on the baking sheets for about 10 minutes, then transfer to a wire rack to cool completely.

Dust with icing sugar to serve.

Krispie Popcorn Squares

Makes 16 squares

I am passionate about children cooking with an adult when they are young. If they grow up cooking on rainy days or to take a treat to a grandparent, they get used to handling food and understanding the joy of sharing. This is a perfect recipe for children.

50g (2oz) butter, plus extra for greasing

200g (7oz) white mini marshmallows

100g (4oz) Rice Krispies

25g (1oz) sweet popcorn, roughly crushed

....

Mary's tips

* *We often use our 18cm (7in) tin as it is good for fudge and shortbread, and makes perfect squares.*

* *If you can't find mini marshmallows, use large ones but snip them into pieces so they melt more quickly.*

* *Can be made up to 2 days ahead.*

* *Not for freezing.*

Grease an 18cm (7in) square shallow tin and line the base and sides with non-stick baking paper.

Melt the butter in a saucepan over a medium heat. Add the marshmallows and stir until melted.

Remove from the heat and add the Krispies and popcorn. Stir until everything is coated well.

Tip into the tin and gently push the mixture down and into the corners, using the back of a spoon. Cut a square of non-stick baking paper and place this on top of the mixture. Press down with your hands to flatten it into the tin.

Place in the fridge to chill for 2 hours before turning out and slicing into squares.

Chocolate Butterfly Cakes

Makes 12

These will never be out of fashion as they are loved by old and young alike. Knowing how children love chocolate spread, you could add a little of this under the butter icing or sprinkle with chocolate pieces.

25g (1oz) cocoa powder, sifted

2 tbsp boiling water

100g (4oz) baking spread, straight from the fridge

100g (4oz) caster sugar

75g (3oz) self-raising flour

1 tsp baking powder

2 large eggs

1 tbsp icing sugar, sifted

Butter Icing

75g (3oz) butter, softened

175g (6oz) icing sugar, sifted

1 tsp vanilla extract

1 tbsp milk

....

Mary's tips

* *Can be made a day ahead.*

* *Freeze well.*

Preheat the oven to 180°C/160°C fan/Gas 4 and line a 12-hole bun tin with fairy cases.

Measure the cocoa powder into a bowl and stir in the boiling water. Mix to a smooth paste. Add the baking spread, sugar, flour, baking powder and eggs, and whisk together using an electric whisk until light and fluffy.

Spoon the mixture into the cases and bake in the oven for about 18–20 minutes, or until well risen. Transfer to a wire rack to cool.

To make the butter icing, measure the butter, half the icing sugar, the vanilla and milk into a bowl and whisk with an electric whisk until smooth. Add the remaining icing sugar and whisk again until pale and light. Fit a piping bag with a fluted nozzle and spoon the buttercream into the piping bag.

Cut out a round shallow cone shape from the middle of one of the cakes and slice the cone in half to give two butterfly wings. Pipe icing into the centre of the cake, then arrange the two butterfly wings on top. Repeat with all the cakes.

Dust with icing sugar to serve.

Paradise Chocolate Cake

Serves 8

This is one of those wicked, indulgent cakes that is perfect for chocoholics!

120g (4½oz) Bournville
dark chocolate,
broken into pieces

30g (1¼oz) cocoa
powder, sifted

4 tbsp boiling water

200g (7oz) baking spread,
straight from the fridge,
plus extra for greasing

3 large eggs

100g (4oz) caster sugar

100g (4oz) light
muscovado sugar

175g (6oz) self-raising flour

2 tbsp milk

2 tbsp apricot jam, warmed

Ganache Icing

200g (7oz) double cream

200g (7oz) Bournville
dark chocolate,
broken into pieces

To Decorate

100g (4oz) Bournville
dark chocolate

200g (7oz) Belgian
continental white chocolate

Icing sugar, to dust

....

Mary's tips

* *Can be made a day ahead
and iced on the day.*

* *Un-iced cake freezes well.*

Preheat the oven to 160°C/140°C fan/Gas 3. Grease and base line a 20cm (8in) deep cake tin and place a piece of non-stick baking paper on a baking sheet.

To make the cake, place the chocolate in a bowl set over a pan of gently simmering water, making sure the base of the bowl does not touch the water. Stir gently until the chocolate has just melted. Set aside to cool.

Place the cocoa powder in a large bowl, pour in the boiling water and mix to a smooth paste. Add the baking spread, eggs, sugars, flour, milk and melted chocolate and whisk using an electric whisk for 2 minutes, until light and smooth.

Spoon the mixture into the tin and level the surface. Bake in the oven for 1–1¼ hours, until well risen and coming away from the sides of the tin. Expect a crack on the top like a brownie. Leave to cool in the tin for 10 minutes, then carefully remove and finish cooling on a wire rack.

To make the ganache icing, measure the cream into a saucepan and heat until simmering. Remove from the heat and add the chocolate. Stir until melted, then set aside in a cool place to thicken to a spreadable consistency.

Brush the top and sides of the cake with the warmed apricot jam, then spread the ganache over. Use a palette knife to smooth the edges. Leave to set for about 2 hours.

To make the decoration, break the dark chocolate into one bowl and the white chocolate into another. Set each bowl over a pan of gently simmering water, making sure the base of the bowls do not touch the water. Stir gently until just melted. Spread the white chocolate on to the prepared baking sheet and use the back of a spoon to make a thin rectangle about 25 × 18cm (10 × 7in). Using another spoon, drizzle the dark chocolate over the white chocolate to make a zig zag pattern. Place in the fridge to chill for 30 minutes.

Once the chocolate is hard, slice into wedges and stand them vertically on the cake. Dust with icing sugar to serve.

Sunshine Cake

Serves 8

This cake is a joy – banana, courgette and carrot are the hidden gems that children will not realise are there! To give added interest and texture, we like to use banana slices or dried banana for decoration. This is not a deep cake, as it has a closer texture than a plain sponge.

225g (8oz) self-raising flour

175g (6oz) caster sugar

1 tsp baking powder

4 large eggs

225ml (8fl oz) sunflower oil, plus extra for greasing

100g (4oz) carrot, peeled and coarsely grated

100g (4oz) overripe banana, mashed

100g (4oz) courgettes, coarsely grated

75g (3oz) chewy dried banana slices, broken into pieces

Cream Cheese Icing

100g (4oz) butter, softened

100g (4oz) full-fat cream cheese

1 tsp vanilla extract

225g (8oz) icing sugar

....

Mary's tips

* *Can be made a day ahead and iced on the day of serving.*

* *Un-iced cakes can be frozen.*

Preheat the oven to 180°C/160°C fan/Gas 4. Grease two loose-bottomed 20cm (8in) sandwich cake tins and base line with non-stick baking paper.

Measure the flour, sugar and baking powder into a large bowl.

Beat the eggs in a separate bowl, then add the oil, carrot, mashed banana and courgettes to the eggs and stir. Add these wet ingredients to the dry ingredients and whisk together using an electric whisk until combined.

Divide the mixture between the two tins and bake in the oven for 25–30 minutes, or until well risen and lightly golden.

Leave to cool in the tins for 10 minutes, then turn out on to a wire rack to cool completely. The cakes will shrink back a little when cooling.

To make the icing, place the butter and cream cheese in a large bowl and whisk with an electric whisk until combined. Add the vanilla and half the icing sugar and whisk again until combined. Add the remaining icing sugar and whisk until light and fluffy.

Spread half the icing over one cake. Sandwich the cakes together, then spread the remaining icing on the top and swirl. Arrange the slices of banana in a spiral pattern.

Cut into slices to serve.

Victoria Sponge Sandwich

Serves 8

This classic recipe is such a favourite. I have included it in this book as it started my love of cooking cakes. For my first job for the Electricity Board, I would visit people in their homes and teach them how to use their ovens by cooking this fabulous cake. The all-in-one method makes it one of the simplest cakes to make. I feel it is the most healing of cakes to make, too. You must be accurate with your weighing, though, as there is no hiding with it – no icing to cover any mistakes! Baking spread should be kept in the fridge until needed. Soft butter could also be used, but we find baking spread gives a lighter rise.

Sponge

225g (8oz) baking spread,
   straight from the fridge,
   plus extra for greasing

225g (8oz) caster sugar

4 eggs

225g (8oz) self-raising flour

1 level tsp baking powder

Filling and Topping

½ × 370g jar strawberry jam

300ml (½ pint) pouring
   double cream, whipped

A little caster sugar,
   to sprinkle

....

Mary's tips

* *Can be made and assembled
  up to 8 hours ahead.*

* *Keep cake wrapped in
  the fridge but serve at
  room temperature.*

* *Cooked cakes freeze well.*

Preheat the oven to 180°C/160°C fan/Gas 4. Lightly grease two 20cm (8in) deep loose-bottomed sandwich tins and line the bases with non-stick baking paper.

Measure the sponge ingredients into a large bowl or free-standing mixer and beat for about 2 minutes with an electric whisk until beautifully smooth and lighter in colour. The time will vary according to the efficiency of the mixer.

Divide the mixture between the tins and level the tops. Bake in the oven for about 25 minutes, or until well risen and golden and the cakes are shrinking away from the sides of the tins. The tops of the cakes should spring back when pressed lightly with a finger.

Leave the cakes to cool in the tins for a few moments, then run a palette knife around the edge of the tins to free the sides. Turn the cakes out, then peel off the paper and leave to cool completely on a wire rack.

Choose the cake with the best top and spread the underside with jam. Put the other cake top downwards on a serving plate. Spread this cake carefully with the whipped cream. Sit the other cake on top (jam side touching the cream).

Sprinkle with sugar and cut into slices to serve.

Coffee Latte Traybake

Makes 12–16 pieces

A creamy coffee traybake, just like a latte coffee. Traybakes are the most useful of cakes, whether they are for lunch boxes, children's parties or for friends, as they are easy to cook and easy to store.

Coffee Cake

2 tbsp instant coffee granules

2 tbsp boiling water

225g (8oz) baking spread, straight from the fridge, plus extra for greasing

225g (8oz) light muscovado sugar

225g (8oz) self-raising flour

1 tsp baking powder

4 large eggs

Mascarpone Icing

1 tsp instant coffee granules

1–2 tbsp boiling water

75g (3oz) soft butter

100g (4oz) full-fat mascarpone cheese

200g (7oz) icing sugar

....

Mary's tips

* *Can be made up to a day ahead and iced on the day.*

* *Freezes well un-iced.*

* *Baking spread gives an excellent result but must be used straight from the fridge. If you wish to use butter, make sure it is soft before mixing to prevent lumps.*

Preheat the oven to 180°C/160°C fan/Gas 4. Grease the base and sides of a 23 × 30cm (9 × 12in) traybake tin and line with non-stick baking paper.

To make the cake, measure the coffee granules into a large bowl and add the boiling water. Stir to dissolve. Measure all the remaining cake ingredients into the bowl and whisk using an electric whisk until light and fluffy.

Spoon the sponge into the tin and level the surface. Bake in the oven for 30–35 minutes, or until well risen and springing back when pressed in the centre.

Leave to cool in the tin for 10 minutes, then carefully turn out, discard the lining paper and set aside to cool completely on a wire rack.

To make the icing, dissolve the coffee granules in the boiling water in a small bowl and mix until smooth. Measure the butter into a large bowl or free-standing mixer and whisk with an electric whisk to soften. Add the mascarpone, coffee and icing sugar and whisk again until smooth and creamy.

Spread over the traybake and swirl the top. Slice into pieces to serve.

Citrus Traybake with Glacé Icing

Makes 16 pieces

If you are not eating the traybake all at once, just cut each square as needed to prevent the cake drying out. Citrus cakes are always a favourite in our house.

Citrus Sponge

225g (8oz) baking spread, straight from the fridge, plus extra for greasing

225g (8oz) caster sugar

225g (8oz) self-raising flour

4 large eggs

1 tsp baking powder

Finely grated zest of 1 lime, 1 lemon and 1 orange

Glacé Icing

225g (8oz) icing sugar

Juice of ½ lime, ½ lemon and ½ orange

Finely grated zest of ½ lemon and ½ orange, to decorate

....

Mary's tips

* *Best eaten on the day.*

* *Freezes well, best un-iced.*

Preheat the oven to 180°C/160°C fan/Gas 4. Grease the base and sides of a 23 × 30cm (9 × 12in) traybake tin and line with non-stick baking paper.

To make the sponge, measure the baking spread, sugar, flour, eggs, baking powder, lime, lemon and orange zest into a large bowl or free-standing mixer. Whisk using an electric whisk until light and fluffy.

Spoon into the tin and level the surface. Bake in the oven for 30–35 minutes, or until well risen and springing back when pressed in the centre.

Leave to cool in the tin for 10 minutes, then carefully turn out, discard the lining paper and set aside to cool completely on a wire rack.

To make the glacé icing, sift the icing sugar into a bowl. Combine the citrus juices in a jug and pour into the icing sugar slowly while stirring, adding only enough to make a spreadable glacé icing. Spread the icing over the traybake, then sprinkle the remaining zest over the top.

Leave to set for about an hour before cutting into pieces to serve.

Banana Traybake with Frosted Icing

Makes 16 pieces

This is the perfect recipe to use up the leftover bananas in the fruit
bowl that are too ripe to eat. If you have lots of overripe bananas,
they can be frozen and then defrosted and used for cakes.

Banana Sponge

350g (12oz) overripe
  bananas, mashed

225g (8oz) baking spread,
  straight from the fridge,
  plus extra for greasing

225g (8oz) caster sugar

4 large eggs

350g (12oz) self-raising flour

1 tsp baking powder

Frosting

100g (4oz) butter, softened

200g (7oz) icing sugar

50g (2oz) cream cheese

1 tsp vanilla extract

....

Mary's tips

* *Can be made up to a
  day ahead. Store well
  wrapped in the fridge.*

* *Freezes well un-iced.*

Preheat the oven to 180°C/160°C fan/Gas 4. Grease the base
and sides of a 23 × 30cm (9 × 12in) traybake tin and line
with non-stick baking paper.

Measure all the sponge ingredients into a large bowl or free-
standing mixer. Whisk using an electric whisk until light
and fluffy.

Spoon into the tin and level the surface. Bake in the oven
for 30–35 minutes, or until well risen and springing back
when pressed in the centre.

Leave to cool in the tin for 10 minutes, then carefully
turn out, remove the lining paper and set aside to cool
completely on a wire rack.

To make the frosting, measure the butter and half the
icing sugar into a bowl. Whisk with an electric whisk until
combined. Add the cream cheese, vanilla and the remaining
icing sugar and whisk again until creamy.

Spread the frosting over the traybake and swirl the top.
Slice into pieces to serve.

Conversion Chart

Weights	
Metric	Imperial
15g	½oz
25g	1oz
40g	1½oz
50g	2oz
75g	3oz
100g	4oz
150g	5oz
175g	6oz
200g	7oz
225g	8oz
250g	9oz
275g	10oz
300g	11oz
350g	12oz
375g	13oz
400g	14oz
425g	15oz
450g	1lb
550g	1¼lb
675g	1½lb
750g	1¾lb
900g	2lb
1.5kg	3lb
1.75kg	4lb
2.25kg	5lb

Volume	
Metric	Imperial
25ml	1fl oz
50ml	2fl oz
85ml	3fl oz
100ml	3½fl oz
150ml	5fl oz (¼ pint)
200ml	⅓ pint
300ml	10fl oz (½ pint)
450ml	¾ pint
600ml	1 pint
700ml	1¼ pints
900ml	1½ pints
1 litre	1¾ pints
1.2 litres	2 pints
1.25 litres	2¼ pints
1.5 litres	2½ pints
1.6 litres	2¾ pints
1.75 litres	3 pints
1.8 litres	3¼ pints
2 litres	3½ pints
2.1 litres	3¾ pints
2.25 litres	4 pints
2.75 litres	5 pints
3.4 litres	6 pints
3.9 litres	7 pints
4.5 litres	8 pints (1 gallon)

Measurements	
Metric	Imperial
5mm	¼in
1cm	½in
2cm	¾in
2.5cm	1in
3cm	1¼in
4cm	1½in
5cm	2in
7.5cm	3in
10cm	4in
12.5cm	5in
15cm	6in
18cm	7in
20cm	8in
23cm	9in
25cm	10in
28cm	11in
30cm	12in
33cm	13in
35cm	14in

Oven Temperatures			
°C	Fan °C	°F	Gas Mark
120	100	250	½
140	120	275	1
150	130	300	2
160	140	325	3
180	160	350	4
190	170	375	5
200	180	400	6
220	200	425	7
230	210	450	8
240	220	475	9

Cook's Notes

Writing this book has given me an excuse to celebrate my favourite joys about cooking and ingredients. I've focused on these favourites in the 'For the Love of . . .' sections within the chapters themselves, but wanted to share some general tips here to help you in the kitchen. There are certain aspects to my cooking that are always the same – I always use large free-range eggs, for example – and certain cooking tricks that are worth remembering.

Free-range meat

Try to buy the best-quality meat that you can afford. British farmers have some of the highest food standards in the world and it really does make a difference. Animals should always be looked after and loved, fed properly and regularly, and respected for the nourishment they provide. I always use free-range chicken and eggs, and would recommend that you do, too.

Sustainable fish

As with free-range meat, try to buy fish that is sustainably sourced – this means it has been fished in such a way that doesn't damage fish stocks by over-fishing and also protects the habitat. It will advertise itself as such on the packet, or ask your fishmonger or at the fish counter in your local supermarket. The levels of fish stocks do change, so while I have tried to include fish that are on the sustainability list, do swap one for another if you have to.

Eggs

Use large eggs, unless otherwise stated – free-range.

Oils and vinegar

I generally use olive oil for flavour in dressings. When frying, I use an unflavoured, less-expensive oil, such as sunflower or vegetable oil. I like to use white wine vinegar or balsamic vinegar for dressings. Occasionally, I use a special oil or vinegar, e.g. sesame oil and rice wine vinegar in the Roasted Duck Legs Japanese Style on page 96, as they do make a difference to the dish.

Vegetarian and vegan

When I'm at home, I often choose to cook without meat. I have included a wide variety of vegetarian dishes here, as well as a vegan burger (see page 154). I haven't called the recipe vegan on the page, because I prefer a brioche bun and these include egg. Plant food is increasinly popular and should be celebrated along with all other foods.

Metric and imperial

I have provided both metric and imperial measurements. When you are following a recipe, it's best to stick to one or the other – particularly if you are baking. (See also the Conversion Table on pages 290–291.) Spoon measurements are level, unless otherwise stated.

Oven temperatures

As ovens vary in the amount of heat they produce, you may need to cook a dish for slightly longer or shorter than the recipe stipulates, depending on your oven. It can be helpful to use an oven thermometer to find out how accurate your oven is.

Scales

Weighing ingredients is so important especially when baking. Use digital scales that plug into the mains, if you can, as these are the most accurate. The battery-powered ones can be slightly temperamental – if the batteries are running low, they can be less accurate.

Bain marie

We have included a couple of recipes that are cooked in a bain marie (Twice Baked Crab Soufflés on page 29 and Crème Caramel on page 211). In both cases, I recommend that you line the base of the roasting tin with kitchen paper before adding the ramekins. This stabilises them in the tray and makes them less likely to slip about and spill. A bain marie is a very gentle way to cook things and prevents curdling.

Ovenproof frying pans and flameproof casseroles

A number of the savoury stews and one-pan dishes I have included in this book begin on the hob and end up in the oven. I tend to use large, deep frying pans, as the ones I have at home are ovenproof, but it would be just as good to use a flameproof casserole dish. So long as it has a lid that fits and is suitable to use on the hob and in the oven, it will do the job.

Melting chocolate

I have two ways to melt chocolate – one is in a small heatproof bowl over a pan of just simmering water, as it gives a lovely shiny finish. So long as you take care not to let the water touch the base of the bowl, it is a foolproof method. For a ganache icing, I heat the cream and add the chocolate, which melts quickly once stirred into the hot cream. I realise, however, that nowadays lots of cooks use their microwave. Just make sure you heat the chocolate in 20–30 bursts and take it out of the microwave to stir regularly; it can be a quick and convenient way to do it. Remember chocolate melts in a child's pocket, so needs little heat.

Index

Thanks to ...

It takes about a year to bring a book together but this year was different. We were commissioned to write *Love to Cook* by Albert DePetrillo and Lizzy Gray from BBC Books in February 2020 but the global pandemic Covid-19 hit and, in March, as a nation we all went into lockdown. A terrible time for so many.

Thanks to my great team – masterminded by the brilliant Lucy Young, pulling the whole book together – we got there in the end. We were all working independently from home and communicating by phone and Zoom, and arranging to taste the recipes when government restrictions allowed. We froze recipes till we could get together and once the three of us were back working together, we cooked all the recipes again. As a team we are bursting with ideas, while Lucy runs the show and makes it all happen. Our treasure, Lucinda McCord, has been expertly testing recipes with us for 21 years (which I can't believe), but has no chance of catching Lucy, who has been my partner in crime for 31 years.

Once we were out of lockdown in 2021, the photographic team got started. The dream team of home economists were Isla Murray, who did the testing, and Lisa Harrison and Evie Harbury, who made every recipe for the shoot, which was brilliantly photographed by Laura Edwards and with prop styling by Tabitha Hawkins. Such a happy, skilled team, and we had a fun day together for the jacket shots. Thanks to Nell Warner from BBC books and Abi Hartshorne, the designer and illustrator, for bringing the book to its glorious finale. And to Jo Roberts-Miller, our wonderful editor, who we have worked with for years and is simply the best.

Jo Penford continues to be a magician and makes me up for photos, making sure I am looking my best for shoots, photographs and for TV. Since lockdown I have realised even more how important she is (!) and wonderful company, too. Tess Wright helps me with clothes that work for TV and keeps me neat and tidy. Karen Ross, Dave Crearer, Sarah Myland and the team at Sidney St, who produced the series to go with the book, all filmed with great safety in the pandemic.

Lastly, thanks to my agents Caroline Wood (at Felicity Bryan Agency), who has taken over with great care and passion from the late Felicity Bryan who we sadly lost in 2020, and my guardian angels Joanna Kaye and Theia Nankivell from KBJ Management, who hold Lucy's and my hands daily. Thank you to all for your support and loyalty.

1 3 5 7 9 10 8 6 4 2

BBC Books, an imprint of Ebury Publishing
20 Vauxhall Bridge Road,
London SW1V 2SA

BBC Books is part of the Penguin Random House group of companies
whose addresses can be found at global.penguinrandomhouse.com

Penguin
Random House
UK

Photography by Laura Edwards

First published by BBC Books in 2021

www.penguin.co.uk

A CIP catalogue record for this book is available from the British Library

ISBN 9781785946776

Project Editor: Jo Roberts-Miller
Food Stylist: Lisa Harrison
Food Stylist Assistant: Evie Harbury
Prop Stylist: Tabitha Hawkins
Design: Hart Studio
Testing: Lucinda McCord and Isla Murray

Colour origination by Altaimage, London

Printed and bound in Germany by Mohn Media Mohndruck GmbH

Penguin Random House is committed to a sustainable future for
our business, our readers and our planet. This book is made
from Forest Stewardship Council® certified paper.